THE ONE-HOUR HISPANIC MILLIONAIRE

All Hispanic-Americans
Have the Freedom and the
Right to Become Millionaires

Ruben Ruiz, MSFS, ChFC

The One-Hour Hispanic Millionaire

ISBN-10: 0-9768199-1-0

ISBN-13: 978-0-9768199-1-2

Library of Congress Control Number: 2005926480

Published By:
Wealth and Millionaire Publishing
311 Cheatham Street
San Marcos, TX 78666
210-573-6827

www.wealthandmillionairepublishing.com
www.onehourhispanicmillionaire.com

Praise for The One-Hour Hispanic Millionaire

"I liked the book because the information/material that is presented makes the reader want to continue reading. Also, the book is one that every Hispanic should own and have as a reference book in their business or personal library. They would truly benefit from reading it."

Juan Dominguez, CEP, RFC
CEO, Valley Wide Bookkeeping & Financial Service, Inc.
McAllen, TX

"This book, like the author, is practical and straightforward on accomplishing your wealth goals."

Homar Bartra, MD
Phoenix, AZ

"Of course everyone wants to be a millionaire but few know how simply it can be achieved—just by following the excellent advice contained in this book. While great truths are often simple, it will require steadfast attention to your goals and to the principles that Ruben Ruiz has clearly expressed."

Ed Morrow, RFC, CFP, ChFC, CEP, CLU
Chairman, International Association
of Registered Financial Consultants
Middletown, OH

"It's time that Hispanic-Americans change their paradigm from laborers to investors—this book shows you how!"

Alma Lopez, Financial Advisor
Chicago, IL

Dedication

To my dad, who taught me early in life that as a Hispanic-American I had the same rights as any American.

To my mom, who was always there when I needed her.

To my brothers and sisters, Roland, Rosina, Rene, Rodney, Robert, and Rhea, who provided me with a challenging and wonderful childhood.

To my wife, Amanda, and my children, Richard and Raquel, who helped with this book and make my life complete, whom I love with all my heart and soul.

Acknowledgments

Thanks to the following Americans who made a profound effect and impact on my life:

Sister Josie Sanchez, my first grade teacher, who taught me that school and learning were going to be fun.

Sister Rosalba Garcia, my sixth grade teacher, who taught me the meaning of respect and courtesy.

Ms. Pinky Barber, my ninth grade teacher, who taught me the importance of world knowledge.

Mr. Jack Farley, my college business professor, who taught me how to make my first business presentation to the class.

Mr. Ruben Bonilla, attorney and friend, who taught me the importance of developing pride and leadership for Hispanic-Americans.

Mr. Joe Morin, friend, who provided me with many resources and the opportunity to network with many business owners and professionals in the USA.

Mr. Doel Garcia, my dear friend from Puerto Rico, who taught me to think big and think international.

Mr. Jack Walsh, friend, who gave me the opportunity and business system to become successful in financial planning and in my future.

Mr. John Merris, business friend, who taught me how to look at my true self from the inside and the outside.

Mr. Mark Victor Hansen, business friend, who gave me the inspiration and motivation to write my first book.

Mr. Robert Allen, business friend, who educated me on becoming successful in the infopreneur business.

Table of Contents

THE ONE-HOUR HISPANIC MILLIONAIRE

All Hispanic-Americans Have the Freedom and the Right to Become Millionaires

List of Charts

Introduction

"All Hispanic-Americans have the freedom and the right to become millionaires."

- Ruben Ruiz, 2004

Chapter 1

The Hispanic-American Mindset

The greatest discovery of my generation is that man can alter his life simply by altering his attitude of mind.

William James

What is the mindset of the average Hispanic-American who wants to become a millionaire? Perhaps a more accurate question would be: Does the average Hispanic-American even consider it at all? The prevailing wisdom is that Hispanic-Americans don't think about becoming millionaires because of the "rules" we are taught in childhood. Rule Number 1: Get a high school diploma and then, hopefully, a college education. Rule Number 2: Raise a family. If you follow these two rules, you will be guaranteed a fulfilled life.

And here's the bigger rule that underlies the other two, unarticulated but clearly understood by Hispanic-American children and adults alike: only Anglo-Americans can become millionaires. After all, they were here first and had most of the control over America's land and precious resources. The truth many of us fail to realize is that the two life goals of Hispanic-Americans are goals shared by *all* ethnic groups and nationalities. But members of these other groups dare to dream of something more. For Hispanics, the added goals of wealth and financial prosperity never even enter the equation. Our grandparents, and even our parents, believed that making it through school and getting married would result in a great life. But what does it *mean* to have a great life? Does it mean having an average income with an average net worth after we accomplish our goals of education and family? Why should we stop at "average"? Why shouldn't our people have the opportunity to gain wealth—as much wealth as we desire—in the greatest capitalist country in the world, the United States of America?

Based on information published by the U.S. Census, in 2001 a married Hispanic-American family's median income was about $40,000 a year, while their Anglo counterpart's yearly income was about $60,000—almost 50 percent more. Why is there such a discrepancy in one of the richest and most free nations in the world? Is it because Anglos have a longer history in America than do Hispanics? Is it because they own more land and have more varied opportunities than we do? Do they have more governmental, and therefore more economic, control? Or is it because our parents and grandparents suffered through years of discrimination that taught them not to disrupt the system? Is it because this lesson—*If you don't rock the boat, then you can't get hurt*—was passed along to us…their children?

Strong focus can take you where you want to go and get you what you want in life. This is a reality of human nature. Unfortunately, if the scope of your focus does not include becoming wealthy, then you will not pursue it. Think about your own life. Has your mindset ever prevented you from exploring or investigating wealth opportunities that could increase your income and expand your net worth? Have you ever discussed financial matters with your parents? What about the idea of becoming a millionaire? Did you believe that they would laugh at the idea and tell you that only Anglos could pursue that particular goal?

If we look at median income by education (Chart 1-1), we can see that the average Hispanic household headed by a college graduate makes $67,165 a year. If you take the median income of $67,000 and multiply that by 40 years, in today's dollars that number would total $2.6 million over their lifetime. Will that average income turn into a million-dollar net worth? If you subtract taxes from that income, you are left with about $4,000 a month to fund your current lifestyle and to become wealthy in the future. While this amount of expendable income is "not bad," it's unlikely to make you a millionaire. Now, *$10,000* a month might be a different story. You should probably aim to get your income level to more than $100,000 a year—an amount that less than 50 percent of 1 percent (.004) of all Hispanic-Americans currently make.

As I said, based on the current median income earned by Hispanic-Americans, you can live a good lifestyle in the U.S. But is "a good lifestyle" really good *enough*? Deep down, don't we want more income and more assets for our families? Most people, if they really think about the opportunities wealth can bring, would have to say yes. But this is the problem: Hispanic-Americans have not been taught to become millionaires.

In order to become a successful millionaire, you need other millionaires to teach and mentor you. You can also learn from books, CDs, seminars, and DVDs. I am the first to tell all parents and their children to get a high school diploma and go to college. College is an important step in expanding your education as well as gaining valuable knowledge for your career. This will help you increase your future income production. College is valuable also because it serves as an opportunity for young people to interact with their peers. It helps them make the transition from childhood to adulthood. Much of their future social behavior is developed during the college years. Confidence, social standing, and future business contacts are all things gained in college that can be utilized in a future millionaire's life.

So, let's get to the "million-dollar questions." How can I become a millionaire? Is it possible for me to make $100,000-$250,000 in annual income? Is one million dollars a year out of my league? You're probably already seeing the truth: you will have to change your mindset in order to achieve the Millionaire Goal. (By the way, for the purposes of this book, the Millionaire Goal means achieving a million dollars in net worth over the course of your lifetime. You can always shoot for an even bigger goal later—say, a million dollars a year in income—but first things first!) Begin by taking an hour a week to focus on your goal and the steps you will need to take to achieve it. Gradually increase your focus time until the idea of becoming a millionaire is as familiar to you as your own name.

You might wonder if you are destined to be an average Hispanic-American, making average income for your family. Ask yourself some tough questions. Why have some Hispanic-Americans who have the same education and social background as you become millionaires, while you have continued making the same, *average* amount of money? Can *you* have a million-dollar net worth? How about a five-million-dollar net worth? Do you believe that those kinds of goals are unattainable—that only certain Americans are entitled to them? If you cling to these beliefs, even subconsciously, you are setting up a self-fulfilling prophecy—one that will surely keep you from your goal.

Right now, let's start the process of believing that you or any Hispanic-American can become a millionaire. It is easier than you think. Begin by altering your ideas of what Hispanic-Americans can do. You might have to live a life that looks very different from the picture that was painted for you. This isn't to say that many of the lessons you've learned from your parents, teachers, and peers won't help you. They will. But you *must* educate yourself on the techniques and experiences you will need to become a millionaire. Start to believe that you have the right to gain wealth for yourself and your family. Then use the power of your life experiences to go out into the world and begin achieving your goals.

Hispanic Millionaire Action Item:
You must first believe that you can become a millionaire; after that it's all downhill.

Chart 1-1

2001 U.S. Census Median Income for Hispanic Households by Education Attainment

Less Than 9th Grade	$18,120
9th-12th Grade (no diploma)	$23,251
High School Graduate	$36,055
Some College—No Degree	$45,810
Associate's Degree	$51,162
Bachelor's Degree	$67,165
Bachelor's Degree or more	$72,284
Master's Degree	$78,902
Doctorate Degree	$92,806
Professional Degree	$101,840

Chapter 2

The Millionaire Mindset

If you want to succeed in the world, you must make your own opportunities.

John B. Gough

How does a Hispanic-American—or *any* American, for that matter—become a millionaire? Is there a secret formula that will help you to become wealthy? The answer to these questions might be obvious to you. On such occasions my daughter Raquel likes to say, "Duuuhhhh, Dad!" Perhaps you're "duh-ing" also. The secret to becoming a millionaire isn't *really* a secret at all. But if you don't believe the millionaire formula applies to you, it may as well be written in hieroglyphics…upside down and backward!

Approximately 1 percent of Hispanic-Americans have already become millionaires, because they have adopted the "Millionaire Mindset." They focused on the goal of becoming wealthy, much like they focused on their more "traditional" goals of getting a high school diploma and going to college. If you set your mind to it and go after it with a passion for success, you *will* accomplish it. That's the so-called "secret." Not too complicated, is it?

To become one of that 1 percent, you may have to change many aspects of your life, including the people with whom you choose to socialize. Why would you allow friends who make negative comments or list reasons why you can't succeed to derail your Millionaire Goal? If you think you can't achieve the goal of becoming a millionaire, then you never will. If you think *I can, I can*, then you are on your way to reaching that goal. Your mind is a very powerful tool and will do whatever you program it to do.

Imagine that you invite your family and closest friends to a party at your home. After dinner you tell them all that you are going to become a millionaire. What do you imagine will be their first reaction? Will they laugh? As Hispanic-Americans, we are often programmed to believe that there isn't the slightest chance of becoming a millionaire. In our heart of hearts, we may even feel that derisive laughter from friends and family is a normal, appropriate response to our dream. Don't you think that's sad?

If you have made the decision to achieve millionaire status, why shouldn't your friends support and encourage you? Isn't that what friends are for? I believe there are two reasons why your friends may not live up to this ideal. One is the "misery loves company" principle. If they can't be rich, why should you? The second reason is that they are afraid that you might forget about them during your quest and leave them behind.

Please understand: I am *not* telling you to forget about your friends. It is just important that you stay focused, because a constant barrage of negativity can delay your progress or even cause you to abandon your dream. Don't let your friends distract you. (And if they're actively trying to do so, are they really, *truly* your friends at all?)

The reality is that we are all concerned with what our family and friends think. We assume that they constantly wonder about where we are, what we're wearing, what kind of car we drive, whether or not we should buy a bigger house. Whether this is true or not, the perception drives our behavior. You've heard of keeping up with the

Smiths and the Joneses? This cliché also holds true for the Garcias and the Sanchezes.

Have you ever heard statements like, "If you hang out with broke people, you probably are broke too," or "If you hang out with middle-income people, then you will be middle-income as well"? You don't want to abandon your lifelong friends and certainly not your family because they don't have the Millionaire Mindset. Just start adding financially successful people to your roster of friends, while slowly disengaging yourself from negativity-filled acquaintances determined to hold you back. Realize that if you stay middle-income forever, based on United States inflation and tax rates, you will always lead a discounted life—living paycheck to paycheck, not being able to afford the things you really want. There is no free ride to living a millionaire life; there is only hard work.

You will have to become a millionaire mentally before you actually become one physically. This does not mean that you can go out and spend all of your money because in your mind you are already wealthy. True millionaires are quite frugal people. It will also help if you begin to understand that there is a difference between saving your money and investing it. Millionaires save money on their purchases and they save money for a rainy day, but they use their financial prowess to find, or even create, many investment opportunities that will increase their profits. Most Hispanic-Americans have no middle- or long-term investment goals. You cannot make a profit of, for instance, 30 percent if you never take advantage of investment opportunities.

If you have a die-hard *buy cheap* mentality created by a lifetime of hearing "traditional wisdom," then you will always think cheap and safe. And if you think only cheap and safe, then you will never have the courage to take advantage of the investment opportunities that are right in front of you. Already, you may have passed on some great opportunities because you were afraid that the cost was too high. You need to change your mindset in order to be successful. If your mental database has no millionaire files in it, you will never become a millionaire.

Once you have a clear picture in your mind of yourself as a wealthy person, you will want to get up early each morning in order to put your new ideas into practice. You are about to take an unknown, yet rewarding journey: the Millionaire's Journey. Every venture into the unknown requires road maps and signs to assure a safe passage. This book is your map to the millionaire life. Are you starting to think like a millionaire yet? Are you willing to plan your life as a millionaire? Do you believe that you will become a millionaire? *I am telling you that you have the power.* You have always had the power. The power lies in that superb organ we call the brain. The brain is as precise as a computer, and you can use yours to achieve your dream.

Hispanic Millionaire Action Item:
Say it, write it, think it all the time: I have the power to become a millionaire.

Chart 2-1

What Will Your One-Hour Hispanic Millionaire Net Worth Be?

World's Best Money Market 25%	Tax Qualified Retirement Plans 25%
Real Estate 25%	Business Equity 25%

What percentage of wealth in each of the BIG FOUR?

Chart 2-2	
What Will Your One-Hour Hispanic Millionaire Net Worth Be?	
World's Best Money Market * %	Tax Qualified Retirement Plans * %
Real Estate * %	Business Equity * %
*** What percentage of wealth in each of the BIG FOUR?**	

Chapter 3

Your Million-Dollar Computer

We are what we believe we are.

Benjamin N. Cardoza

As you read the title of this chapter, you're probably thinking, *I'm not a millionaire yet, so where am I going to get the money for a million-dollar computer?* The truth is you already own one. Your *brain* is the world's most efficient computer, capable of holding over eighteen billion bits of information. I have heard for years that the average person uses only about 10 percent of the capability of his or her brain. Whether or not this statistic is truth or myth, I have no doubt that most of us barely tap the enormous potential offered by this most amazing organ. Even if most people use 100 percent of their brain, it's very likely that they haven't imported 100 percent of the files they need for making decisions to meet the Millionaire Goal.

Envision your brain as your personal computer. The things that you are able to do today in the world in which you live depend on the files in your computer. You can output only what you input. You can output an Excel spreadsheet only if you plugged the appropriate data into the Excel program. If you want to type a letter, you must have a word processor program installed on your computer.

Of course, you must do more than just possess capability. You must also take the time to learn how to use the particular program. Just because you have Excel installed on your computer doesn't mean that you will receive a detailed spreadsheet of your monthly household expenses magically. You must learn how to enter data into the program and then decide the exact data to enter in order to achieve the result that you want. Below are several real life examples of information you input into your brain's computer every day in order to receive the appropriate output. What happens if your file is incomplete because you have not taken the time to find the correct data for that particular file?

For Example:

Input	**Output**
Eat File	How to Eat
Dress File	How to Dress
Drive File	How to Drive
Education File	How to Study
Swim File	How to Swim
Kids File	How to Raise Your Kids
Walk File	How to Walk
Mow Lawn	How to Start the Mower
Love File	How to Kiss
Job File	How to Apply for a Job
Work File	How to Work
Bank File	How to Apply for a Loan

Now, what about all the things you cannot do, or have not learned how to do?

No File	How to Do Your Income Tax
No File	How to Make a Speech
No File	How to Write a Book
No File	How to Play Golf
No File	How to Knit

No File ____________How to Make Tortillas
No File ____________How to Invest in Real Estate
No File ____________How to Invest in Stocks
No File ____________How to Make a Million-Dollar Income
No File ____________How to Own a Million-Dollar Business
No File ____________How to Make a Profit over the Internet
No File ____________How to Travel around the World
No File ____________How to Become a Hispanic Millionaire

The second set of files looks rather sparse. What steps will you take to make them more accessible? At one point in your life, *reading* probably seemed as impossible to you as becoming a Hispanic millionaire seems today. And yet, here you are, reading without thinking twice about it. Why should the Millionaire Goal be any different?

Your computer brain has been receiving files since the day you were born. Everything you are able to do in life is inserted into a file. Your brain can create output solutions from a combination of many input files. The right combination of input files can help you create any number of miraculous outputs, even wealth. (Imagine the files Einstein must have installed in his "computer.") One day soon, the right combination of files might help someone find a cure for cancer. The right combination of files will help you become a millionaire even sooner.

The right file can mean the difference between owning an $80,000 home or a $250,000 home. It could be a way for you to earn an extra $50,000 worth of income each year. A few strategically placed files can be the difference between your being the person giving a presentation entitled *How to Become a Millionaire* or the person paying to sit in the audience and listen to that presentation. A few new files in your brain's computer labeled *financial independence* can get you out of debt completely. Your computer brain can create a small net worth or a large net worth. So before we move on, let's find out what your computer brain is worth to you today. Let's look at an example of another Hispanic-American's brain computer so that you can compare it to your own. After you have looked at this example, use Chart 3-1 to figure out your own worth.

What Is Your Time Worth?

Throughout this book I emphasize the importance of working hard and making sacrifices in your quest to become a millionaire. It's true. Becoming a millionaire *does* require you to give up some of your free time. What it *doesn't*—or at least *shouldn't*—require is burning the candle at both ends every day of your life until you die. After all, what good is having money if you can't enjoy it?

Plus, millionaires usually become millionaires because they work smarter, not harder. As they accumulate assets, their time simply becomes worth more. That's why I recommend that as you get closer to your Millionaire Goal you *de*crease the number of hours you work while simultaneously *in*creasing the amount you earn per hour. Charts 3-1 and 3-2 will help you track this earnings-per-hour journey. Never stop asking yourself, *What is my time worth?* You will conclude that it's worth a lot . . . both economically and personally.

Let's look at George Sanchez who is forty-five years old. He has a college degree and is married to Maria who is forty-four years old. George and Maria Sanchez have two children and a yearly income of $40,000. George has been with the same employer for ten years. He also owns a home valued at $150,000 and has a net worth of $50,000. Since birth, George Sanchez has received millions of bits of information from his parents, peers, teachers, and employers, all of which have helped him arrive where he is today. We can use this information to make the following conclusions:

Age 45 = Annual income of $40,000 and a $50,000 net worth
$40,000 / 2,000 hours = $20 an hour
$50,000 / 45 (age in years) = $1,111 a year accumulation

Now let's compare George's file to another Hispanic-American's file:

$250,000 / 2,000 hours = $125 an hour
$1,000,000 / 45 = $22,222 a year accumulation

Why is there such a huge difference? You probably know some Hispanic-Americans who make more money than you, who have a larger home and a higher net worth. These might be people you've spoken to without ever imagining they could possibly have a million-dollar net worth. You know the answer to the "why such a huge difference" question, don't you? They have loaded their computer brains with more of the right types of files.

Okay, stop reading right now and close your eyes! Repeat these words to yourself: "All I have to do is input the right files into my brain computer." Say it several times until you believe it. Ignore the strange looks that the dog is giving you. The idea of inputting files to change your life is much easier than first trying to create a whole new belief system based on things you will need as a millionaire, such as trust, motivation, and self-esteem. Please understand that you already have many of the answers you will need to accumulate wealth. You will be able to access this information whenever you want to increase your future income and create a more substantial net worth. It's all in your computer brain, and what isn't there can be added. All you have to do is input it.

It does not matter how old you are or how much education you have received. Your occupation, the value of your home, and the amount of your yearly income don't matter either. *Anyone* can take the first step down the road to becoming a millionaire. A decade from now you will be ten years older whether or not you decide to begin inputting your valuable millionaire files. So you might as well start now and celebrate ten years of prosperity instead of ten years of just growing older.

You might not know it yet, but you have already started the data input process. The information that you have read in this book is already stored in your brain's computer. This book and the accompanying Website, www.onehourhispanicmillionaire.com, will serve as valuable sources for the right kind of data. There are several charts and graphs throughout the book that you will also be able to download and print from the Website. The information and tips in this book will help many of you to reach your next financial level. They will also help guide you to more resources that will help you reach your goals, regardless of your current income and net worth. The faster you input all of the information, the sooner you will reach your Millionaire Goal.

Are you a little confused? Do you understand the information you have read so far? Don't worry! As you progress through the book, you will accumulate more facts and tips that will bring the entire process into focus. Here are a few examples of some of the information that you might have plenty of input for and some that you might need to learn more about:

Real Estate: I'm sure you know what real estate is and you might even have some rudimentary knowledge of the subject, but you probably have not found the time to input information on how to acquire real estate and use it to make a profit.

The Internet: Remember when the Internet was new and you didn't understand it at all? Perhaps you needed your seven-year-old to explain it to you. Eventually, you figured it out, didn't you? Well, learning the process of becoming a millionaire is similar to learning the Internet for the first time. When you have an experienced teacher, it is easy to learn.

E-mail: When you see the word *E-mail*, do you think, *why can't I just use the phone?* Well, you probably already know the answer to that. If you don't stay current and up-to-speed, then you become obsolete. You must add new and varied data to your life files in order to create a wealth of knowledge and experience.

See how gaining knowledge and staying up to date on a sometimes dizzying array of changes can help you achieve your goals? The same principles hold true for your quest to become a millionaire. Now that you understand how you can input the information and resources you will need to become wealthy, you can begin collecting data and outputting "I am a millionaire" into the world.

Hispanic Millionaire Action Item:
Input millionaire action files and millionaire-related knowledge files. Delete all of the negative files everyday.

Chart 3-1

Hourly Earnings & Net Worth Accumulator

Your Age Today ______

______ Divided by / 2,000 Hours = $ ______
Annual Income **Earnings Per Hour**

______ Divided by / ______ = $ ______
Net Worth—Current **Age** **Annual to-Date Accumulation**

______ X ______ = ______
Number of Input Files **Number of Output Files** **MILLIONAIRE**

Chart 3-2

Hourly Earnings & Net Worth Accumulator in Ten Years

____
Date (10 Years)

$ ______________ Annual Income — **Divided by / 2,000 Hours = $ ______________ Earnings Per Hour**

$ ______________ Net Worth—Current — **Divided by / ________ Age = $ ______________ Annual to-Date Accumulation**

______________ Number of Input Files X ______________ Number of Output Files = ______________ MILLIONAIRE

Chapter 4

Your Own "Acres of Diamonds"

A wise man will make more opportunities than he finds.

Francis Bacon

Do you remember the story from the best-selling book *Acres of Diamonds?* It is about a man who owns hundreds of acres of land. He also has a passion for collecting diamonds that ultimately becomes an obsession. The man begins the search for diamonds in his own country, and soon he is looking for precious gems all over the world. Eventually, he is forced to sell all his land. The man never finds his diamonds and dies penniless. Several years later, a very large diamond mine is discovered on the man's own property. The diamonds were there all along, right under his feet. The man was so busy searching for riches in other places that he never realized what he already had.

The average Hispanic-American may think that in order to become wealthy, one must venture far from home. You may believe the town you grew up in is too small to support such big dreams. But the truth is, potential wealth exists in one's own backyard. Where is *your* acre of diamonds? Do you already have the resources that you would need to attain wealth? How can you tap local resources to reach your goal of becoming a millionaire? It is all within reach if you develop a plan of action and learn which resources would best meet your needs.

The *Acres of Diamonds* checklist (Chart 4-1) shows you the items you will need to develop your plan of action. You probably own many of them already. Put a check mark next to those items and focus on the ones that you still need. Don't worry if you find that the majority of the items on the list are ones that you don't have. As you continue to develop your business plan, most of the areas will be addressed.

The list will grow and change as you work your way through later chapters in this book and begin putting the tips into practice. All of the charts illustrated in the book can be found on the Website at www.onehourhispanicmillionaire.com. With your *Acres of Diamonds* checklist in hand, you are ready to learn the concepts and strategies you will need to develop your own million-dollar action plan.

Hispanic Millionaire Action Item:
Begin your wealth and success plan of action now.

Chart 4-1

Acres of Diamonds Checklist

______	Computer	________	Business Plan Notebook
______	Printer	________	Marketing Plan
______	Internet	________	Calendar/Planner
______	Laptop	________	Fax/Scanner/Copier
______	Home Office	________	File Cabinets
______	Knowledge of Internet	________	Cell Phone
______	Books-Self-Esteem	________	Home/Office Phone
______	Books-Business	________	Notebooks with Tabs
______	Books-Systems	________	City/County Maps
______	Books-Real Estate	________	Phonebooks
______	Books-Stocks/Mutual Funds	____	Desk/Table
______	Books-Internet	________	Business Checking Account
______	Books-Infopreneur	________	Business Savings Account
______	Books-Goals/Values	________	Audio CDs
______	Books-Business Planning	________	DVDs
______	TV/VCR	________	Digital Camera
______	DVD Player	________	White Board with Markers
______	CD Player	________	Audio Recorder
______	Car	________	Miscellaneous/Additional

Chapter 5

The Richest Hispanic in America

A man can do only what he can do. But if he does that each day he can sleep at night, and do it again the next day.

Albert Schweitzer

Americans are taught that in order to be successful in the United States, one must get an education. If you finish high school and then go on to complete a grade-A college education, you can expect to find a good job, which really means that you can expect a nice monthly paycheck. The "real world" begins when you become a W-2 or 1099 (for commission work) employee. You are paid based on the hours you work. The majority of Hispanic-Americans enter the workforce as W-2 hourly employees.

Your employer is mandated by the IRS to deduct federal income taxes and social security contributions from each paycheck. The IRS knows how difficult it is to send a lump sum tax payment at tax filing time, and they have enough taxpayers who are paying on the finance plan. While you may not like to pay taxes through your paycheck (or even pay taxes *period*), this is the easiest way to get the job done.

In order to become wealthy, you must learn to save or invest your own money the way you pay your taxes to the government. "Deduct" it from your check before you spend it. Learn how to save and take time to research possible investment opportunities. If you don't trust yourself to put money aside each pay period, then have your employer deduct the funds and put them aside for you through your 401(k) or salary allotment to your bank or credit union savings account. Many people are afraid of the idea of that lower take-home net check, but it won't take long at all to adjust to a new, slightly more modest lifestyle.

The secret to becoming wealthy is not really a secret at all. We create the mystery because we are afraid to implement the necessary change in our financial lives. The "secret" is to create assets. You can do this through savings accounts, investment accounts, retirement accounts, and real estate accounts. You can determine your net worth by taking your total assets and subtracting your liabilities. The secret is to transfer a percentage of your monthly income check into an asset.

How do we make something so simple seem so difficult? Americans have one of the most educated populations in the world, and yet we have the lowest savings rate: the average American saves about 4 percent from his or her annual income. Why is this? Americans have been programmed via the media to spend first and save later. We are born procrastinators when it comes to saving money. In fact, many people are so well programmed that they spend money they don't even have. Charging goods and services on a credit card creates an even more threatening demon: debt. I will cover debt later in the book, but suffice it to say that it's one of the worst enemies a future millionaire can face.

The real secret of wealth, the one every self-made millionaire eventually learns, is that you must save a certain percentage of your income every month first. Then, and only then, you can spend the net. A reasonable goal is to start at 10 percent of your paycheck, and live on the remaining 90 percent, an amount that in your new Millionaire Mindset becomes 100 percent. You may have to start with a goal of less than 10 percent and then increase the amount every month, or every quarter, or every year.

There are a number of ways to save automatically each month. You can set up automatic payroll deductions that will deposit money into retirement or savings plans. You can also set your checking account on automatic draft. It doesn't matter which method you choose. Just set up some kind of system that will keep you from spending that money on pricey restaurant meals, gadgets, a new car every two years, or whatever "toy" strikes your fancy. As you monitor your monthly paycheck, cut wasteful expenses, and pay off your debt, you will find it easy to reach your monthly savings investment goals.

For example, you can set up a plan to start saving 2 percent of your paycheck, and increase it by 2 percent every quarter or every six months. When do you stop saving this way? When you can no longer live a lifestyle that's acceptable to you or you run out of money for your bills. Do you think this will be difficult to do? Of course it will, at first. Becoming a millionaire does take some hard work. If it were easy, everyone would be a millionaire! Each month that you increase your savings investment accounts, you increase your assets column (the left side of your balance sheet).

While it may be difficult in the beginning, you have to pass this challenge. You will probably have to adjust your lifestyle and substitute inexpensive life activities. As your assets and income increase, you can adjust again.

As a W-2 income employee, you will save a percentage of income. If you are a business owner, you take your gross income minus business expenses, and save a portion of income too. That is the secret. Your income stream can create all the assets you want: savings accounts, investment plans, retirement plans, stocks, mutual funds, and real estate. You can print out a balance sheet and income statement at www.onehourhispanicmillionaire.com.

Secret Formula: Percentage (%) x Income = Savings/Investment Assets

Let's look at an example. Robert and Maria Rodriguez work as W-2 employees. Robert is a welder and Maria works for the state. Their gross paycheck is $5,000 a month, and their take home is $3,750. They are thirty-five years old and they begin saving 10 percent a month ($375). They also set a goal to increase their savings by 2 percent every year until age fifty. When they reach fifty, they will have accumulated $100,000, based on an average return of 5 percent. If they had earned a 12 percent rate of return, that amount would have been $360,000. You can go to Chart 5-1 to see the range of a $100 savings/investment per month at returns of 2 to 12 percent. You will learn in a later chapter how to invest your savings and turn that $360,000 into a million-dollar net worth.

Here's an interesting truth: once you start living a more modest lifestyle, you will likely find that you need fewer and fewer material "things" in order to be happy. You learn how to substitute free or inexpensive activities for your compulsive spending—hiking with your family, reading books checked out from the library, renting DVDs instead of going to the movies, etc. You will learn that fulfillment doesn't have to come with a price tag—and that realization alone makes the Millionaire Goal worth pursuing.

Hispanic Millionaire Action Item:
Invest 10 percent of your paycheck today,
and live on 90 percent of the balance, which
is now 100 percent.

Chart 5-1

OHHM - Monthly Wealth Builder

INVESTMENT - SAVINGS GROWTH OF $100 DEPOSITED MONTHLY

Time	$100/mo Invested at 2.0%	$100/mo Invested at 3.0%	$100/mo Invested at 4.0%	$100/mo Invested at 5.0%	$100/mo Invested at 6.0%	$100/mo Invested at 7.0%	$100/mo Invested at 8.0%	$100/mo Invested at 9.0%	$100/mo Invested at 10.0%	$100/mo Invested at 11.0%	$100/mo Invested at 12.0%
5 Years	$6,315	$6,481	$6,652	$6,829	$7,012	$7,201	$7,397	$7,599	$7,808	$8,025	$8,249
10 Years	$13,294	$14,009	$14,774	$15,593	$16,740	$17,409	$18,417	$19,497	$20,655	$21,899	$23,234
15 Years	$21,006	$22,754	$24,691	$26,840	$29,227	$31,881	$34,835	$38,124	$41,792	$45,886	$50,458
20 Years	$29,529	$32,912	$36,800	$41,275	$49,435	$52,397	$59,295	$67,290	$76,570	$87,357	$99,915
25 Years	$38,947	$44,712	$51,584	$59,799	$69,646	$81,480	$95,737	$112,953	$133,789	$159,058	$189,764
30 Years	$49,355	$58,419	$69,636	$83,573	$100,954	$122,709	$150,030	$184,447	$227,933	$283,023	$352,991
35 Years	$60,856	$74,342	$91,678	$114,083	$143,183	$181,156	$230,918	$296,385	$382,828	$497,347	$649,527
40 Years	$73,566	$92,837	$118,590	$153,238	$200,145	$264,012	$351,428	$471,643	$637,678	$867,896	$1,188,242

Chapter 6

The Sanchez & Juarez Expedition

There are no shortcuts to any place worth going.

Beverly Sills

Okay, let's get started. We'll assume that you have made the decision to have a million-dollar net worth in five to twenty years. You can adjust your goal at any time. We just need to create the roadmap that will help us reach our goal. In order to help you understand what I mean, let me take the "road map" analogy a little further. Let's say that the Department of Education in Washington, D.C., just awarded you a million-dollar check to finance educational programs. However, there are requirements that must be met before they give you the check. You must drive an automobile from Texas to Washington, D.C., at sixty-five miles per hour, ten hours a day. (The DOE receives grants from auto dealers.) You have one week to accomplish the goal. The drive should not take more than three-and-a-half days. That sounds great, doesn't it? How many of you could do this? Everyone could do it, right? That's what I thought.

Now, what is the most important thing you would do before you leave Texas? Chances are you would get a map of the United States and highlight the main roads between Texas and Washington, D.C. Perhaps you would get more detailed maps of each state you would drive through to learn the easiest routes. Now you have your maps, and you begin your cross-country trip from Texas. All you have to do is read your map and you will reach your destination. The same principle holds true for your journey to becoming a millionaire.

You're probably thinking that there must be a catch. It just sounds too easy. Well, imagine how difficult it would be if you didn't have your maps and road signs to guide you. If someone offered you the aforementioned million-dollar grant and no road maps were available, your task would be a bit more difficult. Not impossible, though. A truly determined person could hire a cartographer to work together with him to draw a map. That's what you are doing right now, following the purchase of this book.

The reality is that you can't simply go to the store and purchase a "millionaire map" as easily as you would buy the maps of the United States. To become a millionaire, you will have to do the work it will take to create your own financial guides. How long will it take you? Well, it depends. It will certainly take you much longer if you try to follow someone else's directions. The roads to wealth, unlike geographical roads, are infinite. Many are currently uncharted territory. Each person's millionaire road map is different, because each person's strengths, resources, and life situation are unique.

Still, without a road map you will not reach your destination, and without directions you can understand, it will take much longer to get where you are going. By the time you finish this book, you will know how to draw your financial road map and how to follow your own road signs. In order for anything to happen, you must have a starting point and an ending point. This book is your starting point. Now let's begin drawing our road map.

Hispanic Millionaire Action Item:
Get all the help and advice you can to begin drawing your map in the next three months.

Chapter 7

The Millionaire Wealth and Cash Flow Chart

Optimism is essential to achievement and it is also the foundation of courage and of true progress.

Nicholas Murray Butler

Your financial health chart is a picture of your net worth. Don't be overly concerned with what your chart looks like today. We have to start at the beginning. Be patient and you'll see what the chart looks like at the end of your journey.

It's time to start the process of creating your million-dollar net worth. Actually, your goal might be more than a million dollars depending on what your net worth is today. In Chart 7-1 you can see a sample of a wealth chart. To print as many copies of the chart as you need, go to www.onehourhispanicmillionaire.com, click on *charts/forms*, and enter the password OHHM.

Your wealth chart is made up of your assets (what you own) and liabilities (what you owe). Take the difference between your assets and liabilities and you have your net worth. Hopefully, you have a positive net worth, but if you have a negative net worth, you can transform it into a positive one sometime in the near future. It is easy to have a negative net worth with auto loans and credit cards and no savings or investments.

Your assets are composed of the following: cash, savings, CDs, money markets, treasuries, bonds, stocks, mutual funds, life insurance cash value, retirement accounts, IRAs, 401(k)s, 403(b)s, SEP-Keogh accounts, pension plans, homes, real estate, gold and silver, and your business equity. Your liabilities include: loans, mortgages, credit card amounts, accounts payable, taxes payable, and any other debts. The net worth part of the wealth chart (equity) is the difference between your assets and liabilities.

Your goal is to increase your net worth to one million dollars or more at a specific goal date in the future. This can be challenging because of two reasons or obstacles. The first is believing that you can do it, and the second is knowing what year in the future it will happen. Create a chart showing what your million-dollar net worth will look like and the year in which you will reach the goal. Then, create a wealth chart for each year between now and the year that you plan on reaching your Millionaire Goal.

For example, create a wealth chart (see Chart 7-2) for 2015. If you show $1.3 million in assets and $200,000 in liabilities, then your net worth is $1.1 million. Now create wealth charts for 2014, 2013, and so on, all the way back to the current year. Then put all the charts in a notebook with tabs for each year. You will review the current year's chart at least once a week. Remember, you have to input data into your computer brain and that is what you are doing when you review the chart.

The next chart you will need to fill in is your cash flow worksheet (CFW). Chart 7-3 shows you a sample and you can also go to the Website to print blank copies of the worksheet. The CFW is made up of income and expenses. Income includes salaries, commissions, fees, bonuses, dividends, capital gains, net rental income, sales, and interest. Expenses include mortgage payments or rent, utilities, taxes, food, entertainment, educational expenses, child care, medical expenses, insurance, vacations, loan payments, credit card payments, and so on. Your Millionaire Goal is to increase the income/revenue side and decrease the expense side of your chart. Sounds pretty simple, right? Your income minus your expenses equals your personal net profit or savings/investment amount. The more you increase your savings, the more money you will have to invest. The more you invest, the more assets you create. The more assets you create, the more your net worth increases and the closer you are to your Millionaire Goal.

Income – Expenses	=	*Personal Profit*
Profit x Savings Action	=	*Assets*
Assets – Liabilities	=	*Net Worth*
Net Worth	=	*Millionaire Total*

You will need twelve copies of your CFW so that you can fill one out at least once a month. Remember to follow up with your wealth chart as well. You will use your CFW to create your wealth chart for the current year. You will probably make many adjustments on both your CFW and your wealth chart. That is good. The more adjustments you make, the more you are focusing on your Millionaire Goal.

You will start to account for every penny you spend because you know every dollar spent cannot become an asset. Use your checkbook and credit card statements to keep track, and make a "cash jar journal" to account for each bit of cash you spend. Your cash jar journal will show you what's happening on the expense side of things. Do this monthly, or even weekly, depending on the timeline of your goals and when you pay your bills.

Since the days before Christ, numbers have been constant. People lie, but numbers never do. If you don't keep accurate records of where your money goes, how will you know where you stand financially? Run your household like a business, and one day you will have a very profitable household. When that day comes, you will be glad of the small sacrifices you made along the way.

Hispanic Millionaire Action Item:
Within the next thirty days, create your cash flow worksheet for twelve months, and your wealth charts for ten years.

Chart 7-1

Wealth Chart—Current

Assets

Cash Assets

Cash	$________
Checking	$________
Savings	$________
Money Market	$________
Certificate of Deposit	$________
Other Liquid Assets	$________
Subtotal	$________

Invested Assets

Mutual Funds	$________
Stocks	$________
Bonds	$________
Life Insurance Cash Value	$________
Real Estate	$________
Investment Trusts	$________
Rental Properties	$________
Unimproved Land	$________
Limited Partnerships	$________
Notes Receivable	$________
Business Equity	$________
Precious Metals & Gems	$________
Annuities, Fixed & Variable	$________
IRAs	$________
401(k)	$________
403(b) TSA Plan	$________
SEP/Keogh	$________
Pension Profit Sharing	$________
Other Employer Plans	$________
Other Invested Assets	$________
Subtotal	$________

Other Assets

Primary Residence	$________
Other Residence(s)	$________
Vehicle(s)	$________
Personal Property	$________
Subtotal	$________
TOTAL ASSETS	$________

Liabilities & Net Worth

Current Liabilities

Vehicle Loan(s)	$________
Personal Property Loan(s)	$________
Credit Cards	$________
Other Short-Term Debt	$________
Subtotal	$________

Long-Term Liabilities

Primary Residence Mortgage	$________
Other Residence(s) Mortgage	$________
Rental Mortgage Property Loan	$________
Unimproved Land Debt	$________
Other Long-Term Debt	$________
Subtotal	$________

TOTAL LIABILITIES	$________
NET WORTH	$________
TOTAL LIABILITIES & NET WORTH	$________

Chart 7-2

Wealth Chart—Future

Date __________

Assets

Cash Assets

Cash	$__________
Checking	$__________
Savings	$__________
Money Market	$__________
Certificate of Deposit	$__________
Other Liquid Assets	$__________
Subtotal	$__________

Invested Assets

Mutual Funds	$__________
Stocks	$__________
Bonds	$__________
Life Insurance Cash Value	$__________
Real Estate	$__________
Investment Trusts	$__________
Rental Properties	$__________
Unimproved Land	$__________
Limited Partnerships	$__________
Notes Receivable	$__________
Business Equity	$__________
Precious Metals & Gems	$__________
Annuities, Fixed & Variable	$__________
IRAs	$__________
401(k)	$__________
403(b) TSA Plan	$__________
SEP/Keogh	$__________
Pension Profit Sharing	$__________
Other Employer Plans	$__________
Other Invested Assets	$__________
Subtotal	$__________

Other Assets

Primary Residence	$__________
Other Residence(s)	$__________
Vehicle(s)	$__________
Personal Property	$__________
Subtotal	$__________

TOTAL ASSETS $__________

Liabilities & Net Worth

Current Liabilities

Vehicle Loan(s)	$__________
Personal Property Loan(s)	$__________
Credit Cards	$__________
Other Short-Term Debt	$__________
Subtotal	$__________

Long-Term Liabilities

Primary Residence Mortgage	$__________
Other Residence(s) Mortgage	$__________
Rental Mortgage Property Loan	$__________
Unimproved Land Debt	$__________
Other Long-Term Debt	$__________
Subtotal	$__________

TOTAL LIABILITIES $__________

NET WORTH $__________

TOTAL LIABILITIES & NET WORTH $__________

Chart 7-3

Cash Flow—Current Income & Expenses

Income

Clients Salary	$__________
Spouse's Salary	$__________
*Self-Employment	$__________
*Self-Employment (Spouse)	$__________
Bonuses	$__________
Commissions	$__________
Dividends	$__________
Interests	$__________
Alimony	$__________
Child Support	$__________
Rents	$__________
Royalties	$__________
Fees	$__________
Social Security	$__________
Proceeds from sales of:	
Securities	$__________
Mutual Funds	$__________
Other Assets	$__________
Other Income	$__________
TOTAL MONTHLY INCOME	$__________

MONTHLY INCOME
Minus (-) $__________

MONTHLY EXPENSES
Equals (=) $__________

NET INCOME $__________

* Net Income After Expenses

Expenses

Housing	
Mortgage	$__________
Utilities	$__________
Insurance	$__________
Taxes	$__________
TOTAL	$__________
Food & Household Items	$__________
Transportation Expenses:	
Loan/Lease	$__________
Fuel	$__________
Maintenance	$__________
Insurance	$__________
TOTAL	$__________
Education	$__________
Medical Expenses:	
Medical	$__________
Dental	$__________
Drugs	$__________
Insurance	$__________
TOTAL	$__________
Taxes (WH & FICA)	$__________
Clothing	
Purchases	$__________
Cleaning	$__________
Personal Care/Cash	$__________
Child Care	$__________
Household Maintenance & Help	$__________
Entertainment	$__________
Travel & Vacations	$__________
Donations/Gifts/Tithe	$__________
Loans & Debt	$__________
Insurance Premiums	$__________
Investments	$__________
Savings	$__________
Personal Savings	$__________
Personal Allowance	$__________
Other	$__________
TOTAL MONTHLY EXPENSES	$__________

Chart 7-4

Cash Flow—Future Income & Expenses

Date: __________

Income

Clients Salary	$__________
Spouse's Salary	$__________
* Self-Employment	$__________
* Self-Employment (Spouse)	$__________
Bonuses	$__________
Commissions	$__________
Dividends	$__________
Interests	$__________
Alimony	$__________
Child Support	$__________
Rents	$__________
Royalties	$__________
Fees	$__________
Social Security	$__________
Proceeds from sales of:	
Securities	$__________
Mutual Funds	$__________
Other Assets	$__________
Other Income	$__________
TOTAL MONTHLY INCOME	$__________

MONTHLY INCOME	
Minus (-)	$__________
MONTHLY EXPENSES	
Equals (=)	$__________
NET INCOME	$__________

Expenses

Housing	
Mortgage	$__________
Utilities	$__________
Insurance	$__________
Taxes	$__________
TOTAL	$__________
Food & Household Items	$__________
Transportation Expenses:	
Loan/Lease	$__________
Fuel	$__________
Maintenance	$__________
Insurance	$__________
TOTAL	$__________
Education	$__________
Medical Expenses:	
Medical	$__________
Dental	$__________
Drugs	$__________
Insurance	$__________
TOTAL	$__________
Taxes (WH & FICA)	$__________
Clothing	
Purchases	$__________
Cleaning	$__________
Personal Care/Cash	$__________
Child Care	$__________
Household Maintenance & Help	$__________
Entertainment	$__________
Travel & Vacations	$__________
Donations/Gifts/Tithe	$__________
Loans & Debt	$__________
Insurance Premiums	$__________
Investments	$__________
Savings	$__________
Personal Savings	$__________
Personal Allowance	$__________
Other	$__________
TOTAL MONTHLY EXPENSES	$__________

* Net Income After Expenses

Chapter 8

The Eighth Wonder of the World

The reward of a thing well done is to have done it.

Ralph Waldo Emerson

Albert Einstein called the compounding of money the eighth wonder of the world. I'm referring specifically to the process of compounding your earnings on investments, and multiplying your wealth over time. Remember, either your money compounds over time as you age, or you just get older without any compound return. Since you are going to age anyway, why not take advantage of those years and make a lot of money on earnings at the same time? Doesn't that make good financial sense?

If you deposited $1 in a bank in the year 1 A.D. and the bank paid simple interest of .005 (1/20th of 1 percent), you would have $21 in the year 2000. But if your dollar compounded at .005 for 2000 years, you (or one of your heirs) would have a balance of $1,182,049,000. That's over one billion dollars, just by compounding. Chart 5-1 shows what happens when you invest $100 a month ($1,200 a year) at different rates of return for different time periods.

Let's look at an example: Juan and Janie Martinez are investing $200 a month in an investment account that is paying 4 percent for the next thirty years. Go to the 4 percent column and thirty years figure of $69,636, which is $100 a month. At $200 a month, the amount would double to $139,272. After educating themselves on investments and returns, the Martinezes decide to change their investment to an account (or portfolio) that has averaged 10 percent over the last twenty years. Now, go to the 10 percent column and thirty years, and we see that $100 a month equals $227,933. Double the figure and you get $455,866. That's a difference of more than $300,000 over the same thirty-year period.

The above example was built on investing/saving the same amount of money each month. What will happen if you implement a plan to increase that amount by 10 percent every year? You will have different amounts to total. Chart 8-1 shows the compounding effect of a one-time investment, or lump sum amount, and what it accumulates. The chart shows the effect of investing $10,000 one time. If you invested $10,000 in an investment account with a ten-year return of 12 percent and you were able to make the same return for the whole ten years, your investment would be worth $31,058.

How does this work in real life to accomplish your financial planning goals? Robert and Janie Vargas sold their first home and decided to invest their $25,000 profit. They are purchasing their second home and maximizing their mortgage financing. They invested the $25,000 in U.S. Treasury Bills with an average historical return of 4 percent over twenty years. Go to Chart 8-1 and multiply twenty years at the 4 percent amount ($21,911) by 2.5 to get $54,778. Richard and Juanita Garza put their $25,000 profit into a diversified portfolio with a historical return of 10 percent for twenty years for a total of $168,188 (2.5 times 10 percent amount ($67,275) (Chart is for $10,000 investment).

Of course, it is important that you understand that just because an investment has ten-, twenty-, or thirty-year historical returns, it won't necessarily have the same returns in the future. Still, you can use the table to estimate your future net worth, return on investment, inflation rates, and future values.

Now, let's make this eighth wonder of the world even easier to understand than it is using tables, calculators, or computers. All you need to know is your current age, and how to divide your projected rate of return by seventy-two. This "Rule of Seventy-two" will tell you how many years it will take to double your money. All you need is a piece of paper and a pencil and you can follow the next three examples. You can download a blank Rule of Seventy-two form at the Website www.onehourhispanicmillionaire.com.

Let's use forty (age), a $10,000 investment, and 4 percent, 8 percent, and 12 percent as projected rates of return. We now divide each of the three rates of return by seventy-two. The calculations look like this:

	72 / 4% = 18 yrs		72 / 8% = 9 yrs		72 / 12% = 6 yrs
age 40	$10,000	age 40	$10,000	age 40	$10,000
age 58	$20,000	age 49	$20,000	age 46	$20,000
age 76	$40,000	age 58	$40,000	age 52	$40,000
		age 67	$80,000	age 58	$80,000
		age 76	$160,000	age 64	$160,000
				age 70	$320,000
				age 76	$640,000

You can see the difference on your rate of return. We can say that for every $10,000 investment at 4 percent it will take eighteen years to double. A 12 percent return will take six years to double, and will take eighteen years to double three times. Now you can calculate the projected net worth of all your investments. Go to Chart 8-2 to find out how many years it will take you, with a $10,000 annual investment at various rates of return, to hit your Millionaire Goal.

Compound earnings really *are* magical. When you double your return from 4 percent to 8 percent, your compound net worth increases four times. When the values go from 8 percent to 12 percent, the values multiply by four again. Now you know why compound interest is called the eighth wonder of the world. And you're probably starting to see how it can help you become a Hispanic millionaire.

Hispanic Millionaire Action Item:
The Rule of Seventy-two will help you increase your wealth faster if you practice calculating your projected returns once a month.

Chart 8-1

Compound Interest

Future Value of Lump Sum—One Time

$10,000

Yrs.	4%	6%	8%	10%	12%	14%	16%	18%	20%
5	$12,167	$13,382	$14,693	$16,105	$17,623	$19,254	$21,003	$22,878	$24,883
10	$14,802	$17,908	$21,589	$ 25,937	$31,058	$37,072	$44,114	$52,338	$61,917
15	$18,009	$23,966	$31,722	$41,772	$54,736	$71,379	$92,655	$119,737	$154,070
20	$21,911	$ 32,071	$46,610	$67,275	$96,463	$137,435	$194,608	$273,930	$383,376
25	$26,658	$ 42,919	$68,485	$108,347	$170,001	$264,619	$408,742	$626,686	$953,962
30	$32,434	$ 57,435	$100,627	$174,494	$299,599	$509,502	$858,499	$1,433,707	$2,373,763
35	$39,461	$76,861	$147,853	$281,024	$527,996	$981,002	$1,803,141	$3,279,974	$5,906,683
40	$48,010	$102,857	$217,245	$452,593	$930,510	$1,888,835	$3,787,211	$7,503,785	$14,697,717

Chart 8-2

Million-Dollar Goal Chart

Investing $10,000 Per Year

Years	6%	9%	12%	15%	18%
5	$59,700	$65,233	$71,152	$77,537	$84,420
10	$139,716	$165,603	$196,546	$233,493	$277,551
15	$246,725	$320,034	$417,533	$547,175	$599,653
				*	*
20	$389,927	$557,645	$806,987	$1,178,101	$1,730,210
			*		
25	$581,564	$923,240	$1,493,399		
		*			
30	$838,017	$1,485,752			
	*				
35	$1,181,209				

***Million Dollar Goal Approximate Date/Years**

Chapter 9

The Five Destroyers of Wealth

The two hardest things in life are failure and success.

Anonymous

As you start formulating a plan to reach your Millionaire Goal, you need to become an expert on what we call "the five destroyers of wealth." These obstacles can derail the best-laid financial plans. Many Hispanic-Americans will reach retirement age without ever realizing that they were victims of the five destroyers. All American millionaires took care of the five destroyers early in their financial planning process. That is the reason they continue to be so successful.

What are the five destroyers of wealth that will prevent you from achieving your goals?

Number 1

Taxes—Paying more to Uncle Sam than is required by federal law.

Number 2

Purchasing Power—Not estimating the future costs of goods and services, and not earning returns that correspond to those increases or in your lifestyle spending habits.

Number 3
Debt Management—Paying excessive interest, which will keep your investment and savings contributions to a minimum or even at zero.

Number 4
Investment Risk—Investing a greater percentage of net worth in one type of investment without developing a diversified portfolio, which will make a better long-term return within your risk tolerance level.

Number 5
Planning—Failing to plan your future goals and failing to calculate your net worth, cash flow, obligations, and purchases (you must plan everything).

We will cover each of the five destroyers in the next five chapters. I will also include a sixth risk. This risk could outweigh the other five risks, because if you don't face this risk now, then you could succeed in becoming a millionaire without being able to enjoy that lifestyle. The sixth risk is known as your physical health risk.

There are two goals I recommend to help you achieve health and fitness. The first goal is to implement a fitness program that will become a permanent habit. (Note: Remember to always consult your physician before beginning a new fitness program.) To accomplish your Millionaire Goal, you will need plenty of energy. Much of the time that you will devote to fitness will be after work, when you are tired after a long day. No matter whether you choose to work out at home or at a health club, you *must* develop a habit.

How many times have you started an exercise program only to give up in a few short weeks? To make fitness a habit, you will need to implement two major action items:

Schedule your workouts by adding them to your calendar up to a year in advance.

Start out with a short workout period and then increase your time gradually.

We will cover your "Success Calendar" in a later chapter, but for now, mark your fitness times on your "regular" calendar or in your daily planner. What type of exercise will you choose? Walking is a good start, because it requires very little equipment. You can add other more complex exercises later.

The best way to accomplish your goals is to work out every day for the next ninety days to six months. After you have established the habit—making it as indispensable as your "toothbrushing" habit—you can work future programs into your schedule four to six days a week.

Go to your calendar now and start writing down your fitness times. Be sure to add a time for each day of the week. For example, if you can start with a fifteen-minutes-a-day plan, your calendar might look like this:

Sunday:	5:00-5:15 p.m.
Monday:	6:00-6:15 a.m.
Tuesday:	6:00-6:15 a.m.
Wednesday:	6:00-6:15 a.m.
Thursday:	7:00-7:15 p.m.
Friday:	7:00-7:15 p.m.
Saturday:	9:00-9:15 a.m.

Depending on how you feel when you get up in the morning and what time of the day you shower, a good easy rule to follow is to work out fifteen to thirty minutes *before* your shower. This way you can still shower just once a day. It's important to follow your calendar. If something else comes up and you can't work out at the allotted time, make sure you change your scheduled time so that you can still fit in your workout.

After thirty days you can increase your time slots in five-minute increments until you reach your desired and comfortable fitness time.

As I said earlier, the easiest exercise to begin with is walking. After all, you can walk in your backyard, around the block, or even inside your house. Just walk for fifteen minutes.

The second major health goal that will help you accomplish your wealth goals is to live a long time. You want to enjoy and share your wealth with your children and grandchildren. The average human being is capable of living a long life, even to the age of one hundred. The typical mortality or longevity tables say the average age is eighty-five and above, depending on what publication you read. Many Americans today are members of the Centurion Club (one hundred years and older) and the number of people living to that age continues to increase. The fastest growing age group in the USA is the eighty-five and over age group.

With proper exercise and nutrition, you and your spouse can live long and fruitful lives. You will need to read and input into your computer brain information on nutrition. Give proper attention to your health and fitness, and you will be able to use your new wealth to accomplish that goal. All the money in the world will not matter if you are housebound or confined to a hospital bed. What is the point of being a millionaire if you can't enjoy a cruise around the world, a romp on the beach with your great-grandchildren, or—who knows?—a rocket ship trip to the moon someday?

Hispanic Millionaire Action Item:
Start your fifteen-minute fitness program today and schedule time for your workouts for the next thirty days.

Chapter 10

To Be a Debt-Free American

One of the biggest factors in success is the courage to undertake something.

James A. Worsham

What kind of debt do Americans incur? More than you might imagine. Ninety-six percent of graduate students carry an average of six credit cards. Graduate business students accumulate the most credit card debt, with an average balance of $11,585, and that figure does not include student loans. The percentage of Americans who live paycheck to paycheck is about 70 percent. And 63 percent worry about their money. Twenty percent of workers wouldn't make their next mortgage, utility, or credit card payments if they missed a paycheck. Statistics suggest that finances play a critical role in 80 percent of all divorces; in fact, this issue seems to be the number one or two reason that marriages fail. The longer Hispanic-Americans are in debt, the harder it is to break free. They must have a definite plan in place in order to get out of debt.

What would it mean to you and your family to be debt free? What amount of wealth accumulation could be made from the interest you pay to credit card companies? Why don't you act as your own bank and pay yourself the loan payment, and save the interest credited to your account? Then, double up on your return by investing the interest you received.

For example, if you average $5,000 a year for twenty years in interest payments, you would pay a minus $100,000. If you invested the $5,000 a year into a long-term, twenty-year investment that averaged 10 percent, you would have $286,000 plus the $100,000 interest savings to equal almost a half million dollars. Figure your interest savings using the Rule of Seventy-two, and you will be amazed at your new wealth.

The loans I am talking about are consumer-type loans—loans or credit card charges that make no investment return to you. Business and real estate loans, on the other hand, can leverage your money to produce gains and profits.

So how do you pay off all your debts so that you can begin paying yourself the interest? The first step is to write out a debt management plan that is separate from your total wealth financial plan. See Chart 10-1, which shows the Garcia family's current mortgage and debts. Chart 10-2 illustrates how the Garcias could plan to be out of debt within four to ten years. If you plan to stay in the same house for the rest of your life, then you can include your mortgage in your debt plan. I will show you in a later chapter how to sell your home every two to five years for a profit and invest in a newer, bigger home.

A mortgage is a debt, but if managed and leveraged correctly, it can produce an excellent return. Remember, your plan is to become a millionaire, and to evolve in all of your investments. Chart 10-1 shows that the Garcias have a $100,000 mortgage with principal and interest payments of $850 a month, as well as $34,500 in total credit card debts and loans. Depending on your interest, you must decide whether to pay more toward your mortgage or toward paying off the high interest on a credit card or loan. Interest will also help determine if you should live in your home for the rest of your life or buy a new home after only a few years. I believe that once you get on track toward your Millionaire Goal, you will want to invest in a new house every two to five years.

Now let's focus on paying off the total credit card debt and loans of $34,500 in a reasonable time period that we can live with. We'll work through an example using worksheets that you can download from the Website www.onehourhispanicmillionaire.com. Look for the "debt management" forms. The first step is to figure out how much more the Garcia family can pay a month toward debt balances. The money will come from their cash flow monthly plan. Let's say they discover that they can cut some of the dining out and entertainment expenses that they incur each month. The Garcias pledge that they will put an extra $200 a month toward paying off their debts. They should set up a plan that will help them pay off one debt at a time until all of the debts are paid in full. They should look at the debts with the highest interest rates and the highest monthly payments. Look at Chart 10-2 to learn what the Garcias discovered.

Based on the above plan, the Garcias would be debt free (not including mortgage) in about fifty-three months, or approximately four-and-a-half years. Now they have two choices for their mortgage. They could pay off their mortgage based on the same plan above, and they would pay off the mortgage in about four-and-a-half more years. If they followed this plan, they would be out of debt completely in a little under nine years. The second choice would be for them to leverage their current savings/investment plan of $1,005 and diversify their holdings. You could divide up the $1,005, or $12,060 annually, into the following: Investment A-25 percent, Investment B-20 percent, Investment C-15 percent, Investment D-20 percent, and Investment E-20 percent.

So the question is: should they pay off the mortgage or put their money into different investments? The answer depends on their total financial plan as well as their goals. If they pay off the mortgage, they will need to make all savings payments to the mortgage for four more years. If one of their goals is to buy a new home, they could sell the house now, and invest the difference in a new home. Or, they could finance the new home with the least amount of down payment, and invest the difference. The real question is: can they make more money (or return) by continuing to pay a mortgage while investing their monthly savings into other investments? Based on historical returns, they should be able to make more returns in other investments than they would by paying off their mortgage.

Here are two more examples (see Chart 10-3): if you invest the $1,005, or $12,060 annually, into a portfolio and you average 10 percent, in twenty years you would have $766,000. If you took four-and-a-half more years to pay off your mortgage, you would have $1,855 a month, or $22,260 annually. If you invested that for fifteen years at 10 percent, you would have $775,000, or a difference of $9,000 more in the second option of paying off your mortgage. However, you would have no extra money within a nine-year period for other investments, which could cost you a lot more. If you kept the mortgage and made earnings exceeding 7.5 percent, you would have about $75,000 in about four years. This is cash that you could use for other investments, including real estate or your own business. The more "liquid" you are, the more opportunities and the more leverage you have for additional investments. If you were to make a 12 percent return, the difference would be about $1,000,000 compared to $936,000. As you can see, there is more cash flow earned before the mortgage is paid off as opposed to after.

There is a second method for getting out of debt. If you qualify, you can pay off your debts faster than you could by using the first plan. You leverage your qualified retirement plan to pay off your debts. Your retirement plan must have a loan provision for this plan to work. While there are others, the two main types of retirement plans that have a loan provision are 401(k) plans and 403(b) plans. Basically, 401(k)s are private sector retirement plans, while 403(b)s are for educators and non-profit organizations that are in the government sector. By having a loan provision, you can increase your monthly payments to help pay off your debt.

Here is how it would work based on the above example: if you have $200 available to pay off debts, you would have to pay tax on the money before you netted the $200. If you are in the 25 percent tax bracket, you paid $62 in taxes to net $200. By using the loan provision of your 401(k) or 403(b), you could pay $262 a month toward your debts, accelerating your debt payoff. When you use the loan provision, there is no taxable event. The other great advantage of using the retirement plan loan provision is the interest. Typically, you borrow at about 6 percent, but they credit your loan amount with 3.5 percent so your net loan cost is 2.5 percent. Use that amount to pay all your 16 percent credit card debts. If you have money in your 401(k) or 403(b) plan, but have not yet maximized, you should work on doing so. We will talk about all tax advantaged retirement plans later in this book. You don't need to be Einstein to figure this out: take 2.5 percent money to pay off 20 percent credit card debt, and invest the difference.

Hispanic Millionaire Action Item:
Write out all of your debts and the date each one will be paid off.

Chart 10-1 (a)

Garcia Family Debt

Creditor	Type	Interest Rate	Min. Payment	Balance
1 MC-1	CC	17.00%	$80.00	$4,000.00
2 VISA-1	CC	14.00%	$65.00	$2,000.00
3 Discover	CC	16.00%	$65.00	$3,000.00
4 VISA-2	CC	18.5 %	$50.00	$2,500.00
5 MC-2	CC	19.00%	$70.00	$3,000.00
6 GMAC	Auto Loan	5.00%	$300.00	$12,500.00
7 Home Depot	CC	21.00%	$90.00	$4,000.00
8 1st Bank	Loan	7.00%	$85.00	$3,500.00
9 Countrywide	Mortgage	7.25%	$850.00	$100,000.00
Total			**$1,655.00**	**$134,500.00**

Chart 10-1 (b)

Your Family Debt

	Creditor	Type	Interest Rate	Min. Payment	Balance
1.	________	________	________	________	________
2.	________	________	________	________	________
3.	________	________	________	________	________
4.	________	________	________	________	________
5.	________	________	________	________	________
6.	________	________	________	________	________
7.	________	________	________	________	________
8.	________	________	________	________	________
9.	________	________	________	________	________
10.	________	________	________	________	________
11.	________	________	________	________	________
12.	________	________	________	________	________
13.	________	________	________	________	________
14.	________	________	________	________	________
15.	________	________	________	________	________
Total				________	________

Chart 10-2 (a)

Garcia Family New Debt Structure

Creditor Rank	Type	Interest Rate	Min. Payment	Balance	Payoff
		With $200 Increased Payments *			
6 GMAC	Auto Loan	5.00%	$500.00	$12,500.00	24 months
7 Home Depot	CC	21.00%	$590.00	$4,000.00	7 months
5 MC-2	CC	19.00%	$660.00	$3,000.00	4.5 months
4 Visa-2	CC	18.5%	$710.00	$ 2,500.00	3.5 months
1 MC-1	CC	17.00%	$790.00	$4,000.00	5 months
3 Discover	CC	16.00%	$855.00	$3,000.00	3.5 months
2 Visa-1	CC	14.00%	$920.00	$2,000.00	2 months
8 1st Bank	Loan	7.00%	$1,005.00	$3,500.00	3.5 months
Totals			$1,005.00		53 months (4.4 years)
9 Countrywide	Mortgage	7.25%	$1,855.00	$100,000.00	54 months (4.5 years)
Totals	Debts + Mortgage		$1,855.00	$134,500.00	107 months (8.9 years)

Chart 10-2 (b)

Your Family New Debt Structure

With $200 Increased Payments*

Creditor Rank	Type	Interest Rate	Min. Payment	Balance	Payoff
______	______	______	______	______	______
______	______	______	______	______	______
______	______	______	______	______	______
______	______	______	______	______	______
______	______	______	______	______	______
______	______	______	______	______	______
______	______	______	______	______	______
______	______	______	______	______	______
______	______	______	______	______	______
Totals	CC/Debts Only =		______	______	______
Totals	Debts + Mortgage =		______	______	______

Chart 10-3 (a)

Garcia Family Investment Savings

Example One—Invest Debt Savings

$1,005.00 Monthly	$12,060.00 Annually	$ 766,000.00 20 yrs. at 10%
		$ 207,000.00 10 yrs. at 10%
		$ 78,000.00 5 yrs. at 10%

Example Two—Invest Debt + Mortgage Savings

$1,855.00 Monthly	$ 22,260.00 Annually	$ 775,241.00 15 yrs. at 10%
		$ 383,150.00 10 yrs. at 10%
		$ 144,830.00 5 yrs. at 10%

	Example 1	**Example 2**
In 5 yrs.	$ 78,000.00	$ 0
In 10 yrs.	$ 207,000.00	$ 144,830.00

Chart 10-3 (b)

Your Family Investment Savings

Example One—Invest Debt Savings

$________ Monthly	$________ Annually	$________ 20 yrs. at 10%*
		$________ 10 yrs. at 10%
		$________ 5 yrs. at 10%

Example Two—Invest Debt + Mortgage Savings

$________ Monthly	$________ Annually	$________ 15 yrs. at 10%*
		$________ 10 yrs. at 10%
		$________ 5 yrs. at 10%

	Example 1	Example 2
In 5 yrs.	$________	$________
In 10 yrs.	$________	$________

* Use any projected return.

Chapter 11

The Invisible Destructive Risk

What we see depends mainly on what we look for.

John Lubbock

There is a risk faced by everyone in the United States. We all know it's there, yet we generally do nothing about it. It has been around for hundreds of years and will be with us forever. Usually, to our dismay, we find out about it in our retirement years. This risk can destroy your wealth and principal, and ultimately cause you to run out of money.

While you are working and receiving a paycheck, you don't have to think about this risk. When faced with its effects, you ask for a raise, or increase the sale prices for your products and services. But what happens when we stop working, and there are no more salary raises, price increases, or bonuses? Your income will have to derive solely from your savings and investments. You will need to make enough earnings to provide you and your spouse with a good retirement lifestyle.

You've probably figured out the identity of this invisible destructive risk. It is *inflation,* a.k.a. purchasing power risk.

Inflation is based on the CPI—Consumer Price Index. CPI is a measure of the average change over time in the prices paid by urban consumers for a market basket of consumer goods and services. The CPI is also called the cost of living index. The CPI represents all goods and services purchased for consumption. It includes food, beverages, housing, apparel, transportation, medical care, recreation, education, communication, and other goods and services. It does not include income taxes, property taxes, or Social Security taxes. It also does not include investments, like stocks, bonds, real estate, and life insurance.

Put another way, inflation is the increases that you have to pay each year for all your purchases of goods and services. We all know that goods and services cost more each year, but we hardly pay attention to it. After all, most of us do receive cost of living raises and bonuses. But what happens when you retire or can no longer work because of injury? Will your retirement plans and your investments provide enough income so that you can maintain your current lifestyle? Will your principal and your income increase each year? If they don't increase, then you could run out of money.

How should you handle the inflation risk? First, let's review the history of inflation through the Consumer Price Index (CPI). Chart 11-1 shows the CPI in the United States from 1950-2000. As shown on Chart 11-2, the average CPI has been about 4 percent since 1950. The highest was 13.48 percent in 1980 and the lowest was -.31 percent in 1955. If your life or retirement lifestyle depended on it, what would you estimate inflation to be on the CPI for the next twenty to fifty years? What will future inflation do to your total planning? What is your estimate? The higher the projection the more conservative you should be. I always use 5 percent in my projections unless the client wants a different factor. I would rather use a higher factor to build my millionaire plan, and have extra money, than use a low figure and project a lower factor index and not achieve my goals. If you make more money than you need, then you can give the extra to your favorite church, university, or other charities.

Let's play a game that helps you really understand inflation on a personal level. Look at Chart 11-3. You can print this inflation chart from www.onehourhispanicmillionaire.com. As you can see, the chart has several goods and services listed with their current prices. Now you need to fill in the blanks for the projected prices. You may not see this as a fun game, but it is a good learning activity. Play the game at least once a year. Inflation is a lot like gaining weight. You gain a little every year, and then one day you look in the mirror and say, "How did this happen?" You retire one day and you look up and say, "What happened to my investment and retirement accounts?" Inflation can destroy your retirement. As with weight, it is very difficult to take off the excess in a short period of time. You don't want to get to retirement and be forced to start fighting inflation. You want to fight inflation now, not twenty years from now.

One good way of estimating future inflation is to use the Law of Seventy-two formula from Chapter Eight. If we divide seventy-two by 5 percent (inflation projection), we get 14.4 years. Let's round that off to fourteen years and use an example like the one that we did in Chapter Eight.

Consumer Prices Forecast 2004—Age forty today

	Loaf of Bread	Postage Stamp	New Car	New Home
Age 40	1.00	.37	20,000	153,000
Age 54	2.00	.74	40,000	306,000
Age 68	4.00	1.48	80,000	612,000

One way to keep up with inflation is to do an annual check on prices of goods and services. You can print copies from www.onehourhispanicmillionaire.com and fill in the blanks each year.

What have you learned about inflation that will help you with your Millionaire Goal? You need to make more than 5 percent a year to build wealth. To be safe you should project making over 7 percent to take care of all income and Social Security taxes as well. We will cover taxes in a later chapter. So it could be said that investments that produce less than 7 percent could be considered negative or poverty rates.

Of course, making a 5 percent return may result in enough income annually to allow you to have the lifestyle you want. Some people prefer to invest conservatively and are quite content to live a simpler life. If you are one of them, by all means put your money in investments that average 5 percent. Just be aware of the effects of inflation and taxes so you won't be unpleasantly surprised during your golden years.

Hispanic Millionaire Action Item:
Your goal should be to make better than a 7 percent return.

Chart 11-1

Inflation Rates
1950-2000

Year	Inflation Rate	Year	Inflation Rate
1950	1.3%	1976	5.8%
1951	7.9%	1977	6.5%
1952	1.9%	1978	7.6%
1953	0.8%	1979	11.3%
1954	0.7%	1980	13.5%
1955	- 0.4%	1981	10.3%
1956	1.5%	1982	6.2%
1957	3.3%	1983	3.2%
1958	2.8%	1984	4.3%
1959	0.7%	1985	3.6%
1960	1.7%	1986	1.9%
1961	1.0%	1987	3.6%
1962	1.0%	1988	4.1%
1963	1.3%	1989	4.8%
1964	1.3%	1990	5.4%
1965	1.6%	1991	4.2%
1966	2.9%	1992	3.0%
1967	3.1%	1993	3.0%
1968	4.2%	1994	2.6%
1969	5.5%	1995	2.8%
1970	5.7%	1996	2.9%
1971	4.4%	1997	2.3%
1972	3.2%	1998	1.6%
1973	6.2%	1999	2.2%
1974	11.0%	2000	3.4%
1975	9.1%		

Source: Federal Reserve Bank

Chart 11-2

Inflation Rates 1950-2000
by Decade

Decade	Average	Cost	2000	or	Cost	2000
1950s	2.04%	$100	$700	or	$14.33	$100
1960s	2.34%	$100	$571	or	$17.53	$100
1970s	7.11%	$100	$454	or	$22.04	$100
1980s	5.56%	$100	$229	or	$43.73	$100
1990s	3.00%	$100	$134	or	$74.67	$100

Highest Inflation Rates—1980: 13.48%
Lowest Inflation Rates—1955: -0.31%
Fifty-Year Average—1950-2000: 4.01%

Chart 11-3

The Inflation Game

Item	Year 2004	Year 2014	Year 2024
Loaf of Bread	$1.00	______	______
Postage Stamp	$0.37	______	______
New Car	$20,000	______	______
New Home	$153,000	______	______
Ladies' Blouse	$35.00	______	______

Chapter 12

The Ninth Wonder of the World

I was seldom able to see an opportunity until it had ceased to be one.

Mark Twain

Who would believe that the IRS tax system could be called the ninth wonder of the world? I doubt you were thinking that! Yet, we have a tax system in the United States that by all historical standards is one that we do need. It aids in the defense of our country and provides benefits to all Americans. Please understand: I am *not* here to debate the pros and cons of the U.S. Federal Income Tax System. (That would take a much longer book than this one!) I *am* here to say that you can either pay more or less in taxes, depending on which tax codes you choose to take advantage of. The IRS certainly won't volunteer this information, so you'd better read it here!

In the grand scheme of things, in regard to our investments and wealth planning, how much do taxes actually cost us? Look at it this way: would you rather receive a monthly income check from a $100,000 portfolio or from a $250,000 portfolio? The answer to that question is obvious. Yet most Hispanic-Americans will reach retirement age with less money than they could have accumulated because they did not understand the tax system.

The following is an example of how the tax system works. Rene and Diane Campos make $80,000 a year and are in the 30 percent federal tax bracket. That means that they would pay to the IRS 30 percent of any additional earnings they make, and they would net 70 percent. In other words, if they make $1,000 in interest at the bank and then report it on their 1040, they will pay the IRS $300 and keep $700 for themselves. While some of your savings and investment accounts will probably be set up like this, your middle-term and long-term investments should *not* be in these types of vehicles.

Let's try to make it easier by using the tax formula. If you look at Chart 12-1, you will see the 2004 Tax Tables. Everyone should be able to determine their tax rate by using the table. What tax bracket do you want to be in—the lowest or the highest? A good friend of mine told me that years ago he asked his father why he had to pay taxes in a 70 percent tax bracket. His father looked at him with "that" look—the "you are dumb" look—and asked, "What tax bracket would you want me to be in—the lowest?" Then he got it: if you are in the highest tax bracket, that means you are making a lot of money! (*Duhhhhh*, as my daughter would say.)Your goal is to be in the highest tax bracket. We will use 30 percent for all examples, because it is easier to figure out quickly.

Eventually, your goal should be to reach the highest tax bracket because of all of your future wealth and earnings, right? First, let's do a few examples based on an ordinary earning taxation of 30 percent.

You Earn	30% Tax		Net Return after Taxes
4%	1.2%	=	2.8%
8%	2.4%	=	5.6%
12%	3.6%	=	8.4%

We will call the 30 percent tax factors, 1.2 percent, 2.4 percent, and 3.6 percent, the tax costs of investing. For the benefit of projecting the future accumulation of our investments, let's use 2 percent as the tax cost (factor) for your wealth and investment portfolio. Since you are projecting into the future, you can use the inflation (CPI) risk factor and the tax factor together for planning.

Inflation factor (5 percent) + tax factor (2 percent) = the C factor (7 percent). So we can use the 7 percent C factor as an average. (C is not as good as A or B, but also not as bad as D or F.) Our goal is to make more than the C average, to break even on all our investment returns. Some investors may find the 7 percent too high, while others may say it is too conservative for those who want to be millionaires. For now we will use 7 percent for our examples. So let's implement our Rule of Seventy-two with the 7 percent average. If you plug the correct numbers into the formula, you get 10.3 years. Round that 10.3 years to ten years. In order to keep up with inflation and taxes you need to work toward making a return of 7 percent or above. Now we can look at an example based on our tax bracket and the figures we looked at earlier.

You earn	4% and net 2.8%
	8% and net 5.6%
	12% and net 8.4%

By using the Rule of Seventy-two we can show the following examples with $10,000 and start at age forty.

2.8%	4%	5.6%	8%	8.4%	12%
age 40- $10,000	40- $10,000	40- $10,000	40- $10,000	40- $10,000	40- $10,000
age 65- $20,000	58- $20,000	53- $20,000	49- $20,000	49- $20,000	46- $20,000
age 90- $40,000	76- $40,000	66- $40,000	58- $40,000	58- $40,000	52- $40,000
	94- $80,000	79- $80,000	67- $80,000	67- $80,000	58- $80,000
		92- $160,000	76- $160,000	76- $160,000	64- $160,000
			85- $320,000	85- $320,000	70- $320,000
			94- $640,000	94- $640,000	76- $640,000
					82-$1,280,000
					88-$2,560,000
					94-$5,120,000

As you can see, the comparisons are of the same type of investment. Both made the same return, and were probably in the same investment risk. The difference is that one paid taxes, and one didn't. You are able to leverage the IRS tax savings and compound your return every year. This is a huge difference. If you can put your money into investments that you don't have to pay taxes on now, your return increases tremendously. There are numerous IRS-approved tax advantaged investments (TAI). Which pot do you want to take income from, the 8.4 percent or the 12 percent? That was only a one-time $10,000 investment. What would happen if you invested $10,000 a year? I will attempt to cover most of the available TAIs in Chapter 20. The important goal for now is to know you can use the tax factor for your portfolio and make a higher rate of return from the same investment. Let's look at another example:

Rene and Diane put their money into several $10,000 investments and accumulated $100,000. They are still in the 30 percent tax bracket and they have learned how to make a 10 percent return on their investments.

Investment	Earnings@10%	30%Tax	Net Return
$100,000	$10,000	$3,000	$7,000

This is the second year they will pay taxes on earnings of $107,000. If they continued this for twenty years, they would pay $200,000 to the IRS. If they had invested the $100,000 in a TAI, they would have the $200,000 in their portfolio instead of in the IRS portfolio.

The second type of tax factor investment is called the capital gains factor. Chart 12-2 shows the capital gains tax factor for long-term earnings. Holding an investment that qualifies for capital tax treatment at least twelve months can provide you with a very profitable tax factor. What types of investments qualify for capital gains treatment? Stocks, mutual funds, real estate, bonds sold at premium, and business equity all provide you with a profitable tax factor. The possible investment returns and wealth accumulations of each will be discussed separately in this book. Qualified dividends now receive capital gains tax rates.

As long as you hold on to the qualified investments for at least a year you will qualify for long-term capital gains tax treatment. For example, if you buy a real estate property for $10,000 and sell it one year and one day later for $15,000, your capital gains tax, if you are in the 25 percent or higher tax bracket, would be 15 percent of $5,000, or $750; you net $14,250. If you are in the 15 percent or lower tax bracket, your capital gains tax is 5 percent of $5,000, which is $250; you net $14,750.

If you sold the property in less than twelve months, your tax factor would be taxed at ordinary rates of 30 percent. However, your annual return can be in the double digits.

Hispanic Millionaire Action Item:
You have a choice: you can contribute more to the IRS, or the IRS can contribute more to you.

Chart 12-1

Tax Tables

Tax Bracket	2005 Single	2005 Joint
10%	$7,300 or less	$14,600 or less
15%	$7,300-$29,700	$14,600-$59,400
25%	$29,700-$71,950	$59,400-$119,950
28%	$71,950-$150,150	$119,950-$182,800
33%	$150,150-$326,450	$182,800-$326,450
35%	$326,450 or more	$326,450 or more

Chart 12-2

Tax Tables-Capital Gains and Qualified Dividends

After May 5, 2003

Long-Term Capital Gains & Qualified Dividends

Tax Bracket	Tax Rate
25% or Higher	15%
15% or Lower	5%

Chapter 13

The Emotional Risk

Many people have the ambition to succeed; they may even have the special aptitude for the job. And yet they do not move ahead. Why? Perhaps they think that since they can master the job, there is no need to master themselves.

John Stevenson

The fourth destroyer of wealth is simply your emotions and how they affect the investment portfolio you start and manage. More return on investment is lost each year or every few years, because people make decisions to buy or sell based on emotions. Before we go any further, let's clarify what you might be getting emotional *about.* Investments can make earnings for you in two ways: income while you hold the investment, and profit/loss when you sell it. Got it? Good.

Now, let's start at the beginning. What are you really investing in? It has to be our country, the United States of America. When you put your money in any American investment, you are really investing in the U.S. free enterprise or capitalistic system. If the United States of America were to go under, either from a war or an economic catastrophe, then *all* investments would be worthless. That means everything: your FDIC savings accounts and CDs, treasury bills, treasury bonds, treasury notes, U.S. government bonds, corporate bonds, stocks, mutual funds, REITS, real estate, public corporations, and private business.

Sure, this is a sobering thought. But what else are you going to invest in? While governments from all over the world have changed over the last two thousand years, there is no logical reason to believe that the United States will go into bankruptcy in our lifetime. I believe that the purpose of all human life is to move forward, to be positive, to expect and hope for the best. So my advice to you is to conclude that the U.S. will be around for centuries to come, and only your investment decision will affect your returns. It's a leap of faith…but so is getting out of bed every morning.

There are two major types of investments in the United States: debt and equity investments. You may be thinking, *Who would invest in debt investments? That sounds like a problem or a loan.* Even though you don't hear the term "debt investment," it does exist. Debt investments are sold as treasury bills, CDs, and bonds. That is why there are credit ratings assigned to public corporations—because the corporations borrow money from the public. When you invest in a certificate of deposit (CD), you are actually lending your money to the bank, and the bank is promising to pay back your principal and a certain interest rate or return. When you invest in U.S. treasury bills or bonds, you lend the U.S. government money to be repaid over a short- or long-term period. When you lend money to public corporations like Microsoft, GE, and Wal-Mart, they promise to pay you back the principal and the interest. The interest rate they pay you is determined by the time period and by the risk of the bonds.

Now let's go to the other side and discuss equity investments. If you guessed that equity investments mean you own something, you'd be right. You own a percentage of the investment. Equity investments can pay dividends (income) and then a profit once they're sold. Equity investments include real estate, stocks, mutual funds real estate investments trusts (REITS), a business, gold and silver, and even collectibles. When you invest in an equity investment, you own a percentage of that investment. That means that you get a percentage of whatever income or profits it makes. Real estate and businesses are two equity investments that you can: (1) own 100 percent, (2) have liabilities, or (3) control decision making. They will be described separately in a later chapter.

Let's look at an example of debt (bond) and equity (stocks) investments using a rental real estate property for purposes of comparison. (Please note we are not comparing real estate here.) This example can show you how debt and equity investments have worked in the past, and may reveal your risk tolerance. You buy two rental properties for $50,000 each. One property is on the north side (NS) and the other one is on the south side (SS). See Chart 13-1.

NS Property—rents for $500 a month. For the next twenty years, there is no vacancy, and you collect $500 each month.

SS Property—also rents for $500 a month, but for the next twenty years there is a vacancy rate of 15 percent (no rental income). However, every two years there is an increase in the rent, so by the end of twenty years the rent is up to $1,200 a month.

You can now sell both properties. You sell property NS for $50,000, so you get what you invested (your money back), and your twenty years of rental income. You sell SS for $150,000, and so your profit is $100,000 plus the rental income. Which would you rather own, NS or SS? Well, if I had described to you investment NS only, you probably would have bought that investment. But after explaining investment SS, and comparing both, you would have bought SS—right?

Many Hispanic-Americans might not want to have a rental property that is vacant 15 percent of the time. They want a guaranteed income every month. But the scenario above happens all the time. The choice really comes down to short-term verses long-term investing. Can you handle two months vacancy ratio every year? Sure you can if you understand planning and risk diversification.

There is a way to get a combination of both types of rental properties. It's called diversification, asset allocation, and the optimum asset allocation strategy. That said, we will now discuss using equity and debt investments through the greatest money market in the world: the U.S. stock market. We like the advantages of debt (bond) investments because of their payback of income, almost on a guaranteed basis. The resale value of such investments is usually always the same, and we can get our money back fast by selling them. What we don't like is that no appreciation builds up, only the reinvestment of the income generated. On the equity investment side, we love the appreciation of our ownership of that investment. We *don't* like the fact that there's no guarantee of steady income, or the fact that its market value can go down.

As I mentioned earlier, we can do a combination of both. It's called diversification. Look at Chart 13-2; you will see that the vertical line (top to bottom) is the earnings/return line. And the horizontal line (left to right) is the risk line, showing several investments and risk tolerance. We have also drawn a line across the 7 percent return line, to show our goal as millionaires is to be above inflation and taxes. Each investor must choose one or more asset allocation portfolios that match his risk level and are above the 7 percent line. Chart 13-3 shows the same chart, but here it's divided into four quadrants marked NW (northwest), NE (northeast), SW (southwest), and SE (southeast). Many economists and investment advisors have constantly recommended or subscribe to the portfolio theory, which says to have your portfolio somewhere in the NW quadrant. Somewhere out there is the perfect portfolio for you.

Your greatest fear or risk based on past history will come from the media and the word of mouth of your friends. Please understand that newspapers, magazines, radio, and television news sell emotions—primarily bad news, crisis news, negative way of life news. Why?

Because Americans want to know the worst that is happening in their neighborhood, city, state, and country. Americans are addicted to bad news media, because of our morbid fascination with it. It usually affects us in some way. Negative news about the investment market affects our investment plans, or keeps us from doing any investing at all because we think it's a bad market.

The many millions of images and sound bites that hit average Americans can affect their investment decisions. For example, Morningstar did a study on 219 growth funds over a five-year period ending May 31, 1994. The growth funds averaged 12.5 percent during that time period. That means that if you had invested $100,000 at the beginning of the period, you would have had almost $200,000 at the end of the period. But the average investor in the growth funds during that five-year period had a -2.2 percent return or about $90,000 in their portfolios. That is a difference of about $110,000.

Why? you might be asking. *Why? Why? Why? Why?* You may as well ask why a man does what he does when he is falling in love. It's all about emotion. These investors made -2.2 percent because they did not leave their money in those funds for five years. They "sold out" at the wrong time and took a loss. Maybe it was the media, or their quarterly statement, or their peers—whatever the reason, they did not stay the course. Quite simply, their emotions made them sell.

Do your emotions affect you when you are filing your 1040 tax return? Sure they do, but unless you're willing to risk jail time, you pay the IRS anyway. Why? Because there's not a damn thing you can do about it. Take the same attitude with your portfolio. Don't worry about your emotions. Look at the long-term, not at the short-term. Then, ten or twenty years down the line, you can say of the market's ups and downs, "Well, there was not a damn thing I could do about it!" By then these "hiccups" won't matter anyway, because you will have made a great return!

Hispanic Millionaire Action Item:
Believe in the United States of America and invest monthly.

Chart 13-1

Debt vs. Equity

Comparison Using a Rental House

		NS House		**SS House**
Invest		$50,000		$50,000
Rental		$6,000 a year for 20 years		$6,000 a year & increases for 20 years 15% vacancy ratio
Total Rental Income	=	$120,000	=	$173,000
Sell	=	$50,000	=	$150,000
Total	=	$170,000	=	$323,000

Please note: this is not a real estate comparison but an example of how debt and equity investments work with a rental house as an easier example to understand.

Chart 13-2

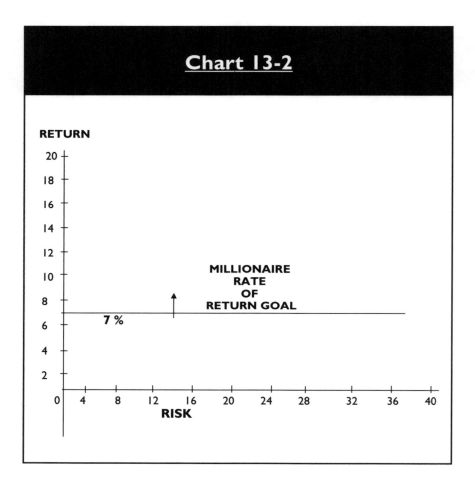

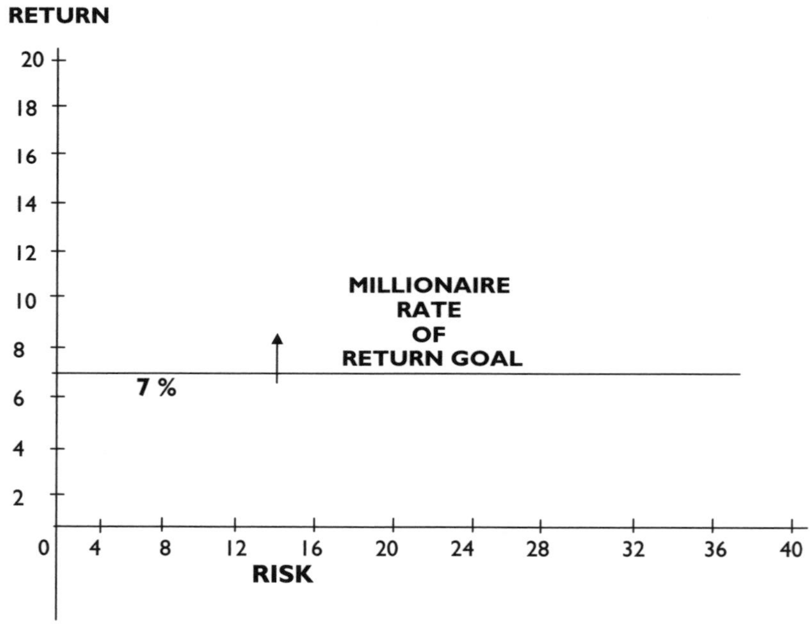
RETURN
20
18
16
14
12
10
8
6
4
2
0
4
8
12
16
20
24
28
32
36
40
RISK
MILLIONAIRE
RATE
OF
RETURN GOAL
7 %

Chart 13-3

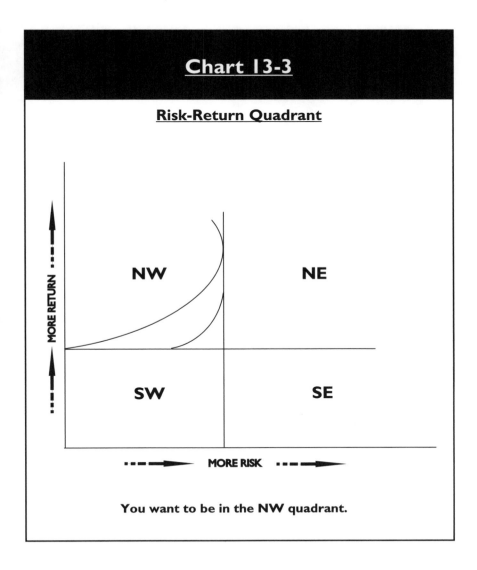

Risk-Return Quadrant

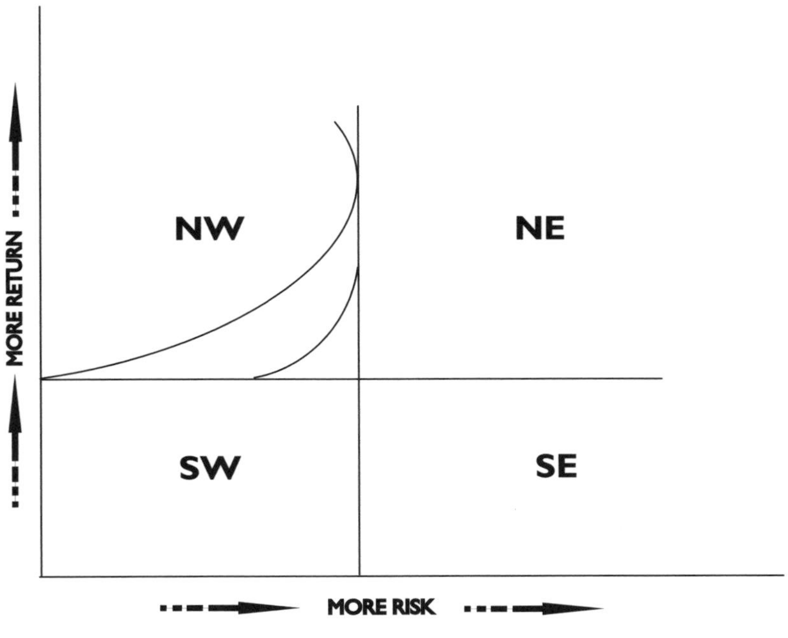

You want to be in the NW quadrant.

Chapter 14

The "P" Word—the Greatest Risk of All

It takes time to succeed because success is merely the natural reward for taking time to do anything well.

Joseph Ross

So far, I've talked quite a bit about the "R" word: risk. Now, I would like to summarize my thoughts on the subject. All wealth goals come with risks. That includes the goal of becoming a millionaire. But here is the bigger truth: there are risks for everything we do in life. The key lies in learning how to counteract those risks. We protect our families by providing shelter and teaching them our values. We get our children immunized so they'll be less likely to get sick. We take out insurance policies to protect ourselves and those we love in the event of catastrophe.

Yes, there are risks all around us, but we combat those risks by educating ourselves and by taking action. There is no difference regarding the quest to become a millionaire through multiple investment plans. There are inflation risks, debt risks, tax risks, as well as diversification and emotional risks that have an effect on wealth investing. And there is another risk that probably has the greatest impact on your financial planning goals. It is the "not planning" risk. You can't become a millionaire without putting some work or effort into the goal. There are no short cuts. You won't develop wealth without investing or taking some other action.

Planning, or the "P" word, is the essence of success. It is knowledge that creates the resources that give you the power to take action. It is the power to find out what inflation, debt, taxes, diversification, and emotion can do for your personal success goals. You must create your financial goals, and you must use every resource and professional available to help you succeed.

Planning will require you to write out your goals. Most people don't like to write out goals—maybe they were never taught how. Then they have to read those goals at least weekly, if not daily, until they become very clear. When your goals are clear and you implement steps to reach them, action and results follow.

Don't be afraid of success. But do understand that you will have to make changes in your life. As you plan and set goals, you will realize that you may have to miss some of your *normal* weekly activities: Sunday football games, PTA meetings, some kids' activities, lawn work, or golf game. While these activities are certainly important, if you allow such activities to fill up *all* your free time every week, you will never accomplish your bigger goals for you and your family.

You need to get on the positive goal track. Once you start planning and meeting goals, your successes will help you concentrate all your power, energy, and talent to reach your millionaire destination. You will naturally receive the enthusiasm you need to get to the next stage. Your goals will help you develop confidence in yourself, and build your self-esteem. Writing down your goals will help you make the right decisions for your wealth building. Your goal plan will produce opportunities for you that you never would have seen if you didn't have a plan. Finally, your plan will give you the impetus to overcome any obstacles that get in front of your goals. Chart 14-1 is your start in setting up your goals. You can write them out monthly, quarterly, semi-annually, or yearly. The more you write, the better you get at reaching your goals.

Almost all Americans, Hispanic-Americans in particular, do not know how to build wealth. They could double or even triple their net worth by planning more and learning all areas of building wealth.

Let me tell you a story about how planning can work for you. Rodney and Leslie Sanchez were given the opportunity to own a business in the communication industry. Besides the minimum capital the Sanchezes would need, the owners said they would also have to pass a test designed to make sure they had the "right stuff" to run a successful business. They were given a list of ten items that they had to find in different locations around the city. Each item came with a sophisticated clue that told Mr. and Mrs. Sanchez where the items could be found. They followed each clue meticulously until they located each item. They planned after they found each item, until they reached number ten, or until they became successful with their plan.

When you read this story, can you see how planning relates to success? A plan serves as a detailed report that gets you to the next step in your goal. More planning gets you to the next action item required for success. You take it one step at a time. Most Hispanic-Americans never get to the first clue because they don't know where to look for the resources, or they don't want to take the time to sit down and put their new resources into action. Don't neglect the power of planning. It truly is a valuable key to reaching your Millionaire Goal.

Hispanic Millionaire Action Item:
Every day, week, month, and year,
plan, plan, and plan some more.

Chart 14-1

Planning

Short-Term Goals—Next 12 Months

____
____
____
____
____
____
____
____

Middle-Term Goals—Next 1–5 Years

____
____
____
____
____
____
____
____

Long-Term Goals—Next 10 or More Years

____
____
____
____
____
____
____
____

Chapter 15

The One-Hour Hispanic Millionaire

I am not the smartest or most talented person in the world, but I succeeded because I keep going, and going, and going.

Sylvester Stallone

The first fourteen chapters of this book gave you the conditions and obstacles that Hispanic-Americans have to overcome in order to become successful. You should read those chapters over again, many times, and create an outline based on them. You can now use this outline to create your own business operations manual. You have probably worked for a company that has an operations manual, a document that tells all employees what they should and should not do. Who do you think created the operations manual? Someone like you created it—and there is no one better suited to create this one.

The next fifteen chapters will focus on helping you create your successful O*ne-Hour Hispanic Millionaire* plan of action. Your plan of action will be added to your outline, and could be as little as one page or as many as ten pages—each person's will be different. We will start where we ended in Chapter 14, with *planning*. You will begin by setting aside one hour a week to build your success plan, and then eventually you will spend one hour a day.

Your one hour a week is very important for your financial success. I realize that you are probably very busy. (Hey, who isn't?) This means that you need to begin with a reasonable amount of time that you can stick with. One hour a week is a goal that all Hispanic-Americans, no matter how busy, can achieve. And the act of setting aside that one hour a week allows you to focus all your attention on becoming a millionaire. Chart 15-1 shows you how to set aside your *One-Hour Hispanic Millionaire* hour for the next fifty-two weeks.

To get started you should do the following steps as soon as you can:

1. Set up your one-hour planning (OHP) sessions for when you have the most rest and the least stress. This could be in early morning, just before bed, or anytime on Saturday or Sunday.
2. Set up your OHP in a place where there is no distraction from family or others.
3. If both you and your spouse are doing the OHP, you can either set up separate times or the same hour and location for both of you. If you set up separate times, you might want to allow one session a month for going over each other's plans.
4. Whatever time and day you set, keep the appointment with yourself, like you would a doctor's appointment. DON'T MISS IT. Treat this appointment as though it is critical to your and your family's well-being—because it is.
5. Get a binder with tabs and paper covering all the topics, goals, and obstacles covered in this book. (You can also set it up in your computer.)
6. Create a checklist for everything you are planning to do. (See sample Chart 16-1, which can be printed from the Website—www.onehourhispanicmillionaire.com.) You will need a calendar that includes daily, weekly, monthly, and annual dates, as well as a five-year calendar.
7. You will need an outline of your business and action plans.

8. You will need your net worth wealth chart and each flow management worksheet.
9. You will need your short-, medium-, and long-term goal sheets.

Now you are ready to initiate your action plan by learning how to create new assets, increase your net worth, choose appropriate investments, protect your assets, diversify your assets, and leverage and manage your time. Good luck. Here's where the journey really begins!

Hispanic Millionaire Action Item:
Get your binder and set up your weekly planning time.

Chart 15-1

The One-Hour Hispanic Millionaire Hour

Week	Sunday	Monday	Tuesday	Wednesday	Thursday	Friday	Saturday
Week 1	7:00 pm						
Week 2	7:00 pm						
Week 3							10:00 am
Week 4				12:00 pm			
Week 5							6:00 pm
Week 6	6:00 pm						
Week 7			12:00 pm				
Week 8						8:00 pm	
Week 9		6:00 am					
Week 10					7:00 pm		
Week 11							9:00 am
Week 12	4:00 pm						
Week 13				4:00 pm			
Week 14		6:00 pm					
Week 15						6:00 pm	
Week 16	6:00 pm						
Week 17							1:00 pm
Week 18			5:00 pm				
Week 19				5:00 pm			
Week 20						7:00 pm	
Week 21		7:00 pm					
Week 22		12:00 pm					
Week 23			8:00 am				
Week 24	8:00 pm						
Week 25					3:00 pm		
Week 26		1:00 pm					
Week 27			1:00 pm				
Week 28						7:00 pm	
Week 29						7:00 pm	
Week 30							8:00 am
Week 31	7:00 pm						
Week 32		8:00 am					
Week 33						5:00 pm	
Week 34				7:00 pm			
Week 35				7:00 pm			
Week 36							5:00 pm
Week 37							5:00 pm
Week 38	12:00 pm						
Week 39				5:00 pm			
Week 40		8:00 am					
Week 41		8:00 am					
Week 42						5:00 pm	
Week 43							8:00 am
Week 44				5:00 pm			
Week 45							10:00 am
Week 46	8:00 pm						
Week 47			6:00 pm				
Week 48							
Week 49				6:00 pm			
Week 50							12:00 pm
Week 51		8:00 pm					
Week 52	7:00 pm						

Chapter 16

The Miracle of Your Calendar

The secret to success in life is for a man to be ready for his opportunity when it comes.

Benjamin Disraeli

Your calendar will become the focus, the essence, the *miracle* of your successful millionaire action plan. How can a calendar be a miracle? Well, a funny thing happens when you write an appointment or event down: you actually do it! When that appointment allows you to change what you do so that your financial reality moves from mediocre to millionaire, well, wouldn't *you* call that a miracle?

You are probably thinking that you can't possibly take time out of your hectic schedule to set up a calendar. If you're not thinking that, you will be in a minute when you see how detailed I'm asking you to make it! But if you continue doing what you have been doing for the past five years—living *without* a millionaire calendar—where will it get you? Basically, it will get you where you are right now. Slowly but surely, you have to make a "wealth change," and your calendar is the beginning.

Before you actually set up your calendar, take time to review what goes on in your normal twenty-four-hour day. Go to Chart 16-

2 and fill in the things that you do during the day, following the example shown in Chart 16-1. Fill out each time slot with the following duties and events: sleeping and eating habits, your daily commute, the number of hours you work, your family obligations, any social activities, and the chores that you do around the house. Do one chart for the activities that you do Monday through Friday and another chart for Saturday and Sunday. Do you run out of time every day? Can you take some time from your leisure activities and use that time for your millionaire activities?

The first item you should put on your calendar is your one-hour appointment with yourself to plan your financial goals and actions. Write down the one-hour meetings for the next fifty-two weeks (Chart 15-1). Yes, all fifty-two weeks. Don't say you will do the rest of the weeks later. Just do it now. Your one-hour meetings can be on different days of the week. Next, you will write out the following on Chart 16-3:

Work Time
Commute Time
Eating Time
Sleep Time
Morning Routine Time
Personal Time

All of the above time slots can now be filled in around your weekly one-hour planning sessions, until you are done. While writing out what you will do in the future is one of the most difficult tasks in the wealth-building process, there is no other way. Of course, you will have unavoidable changes in your schedule because of work events, sick children, and other personal matters, but as long as you get your "millionaire hour" in sometime during the week, you'll stay on track.

By the time you have allotted a planning session for all fifty-two weeks, you will have a full year of work ahead of you. As each week approaches and your schedule begins to "firm up," you can fill in the time for your vacations, special weekend plans, and holiday events. This will, no doubt, require some coordination with your spouse.

You didn't know you were that busy, did you? By having your calendar in front of you at your weekly one-hour meetings, you can start to make important changes in your schedule to fit your financial success goals. There will probably be some social or holiday events that you will have to miss in order to accomplish your wealth goals.

Don't forget to add important contacts and other resource information on your calendar. For instance, add your Master Mind team members, which will be covered later on in the book. Take your calendar with you wherever you go. If you're having trouble visualizing what your calendar might look like, there is a sample calendar you can print out at www.onehourhispanicmillionaire.com.

I hope this helps you to see the benefits of getting more structured. Before long, you will see the fruits of your labor really starting to pay off.

Hispanic Millionaire Action Item:
Go to your calendar and fill in all of your daily activities.

Chart 16-1

Time Management Hours (example)

***Workdays (Monday-Friday)**

Activities	Hours
Sleep	8
Morning Routine	1
Commute	2
Work	8
Meals	2
Personal Time	3
Total	**24**

***Weekends (Saturday-Sunday)**

Activities	Hours
Sleep	9
Morning Routine	2
Errands	6
Meals	3
Personal Time	4
Total	**24**

Chart 16-2

Time Management Hours

***Workdays (Monday-Friday)**

Activities	Hours
Sleep	______
Morning Routine	______
Commute	______
Work	______
Meals	______
Personal Time	______
Total	24

***Weekends (Saturday-Sunday)**

Activities	Hours
Sleep	______
Morning Routine	______
Errands	______
Meals	______
Personal Time	______
Total	24

Chart 16-3

OHHM Calendar

Time	Sunday	Monday	Tuesday	Wednesday	Thursday	Friday	Saturday
12:00 am	Sleep	Sleep	Sleep	Sleep	Sleep	Sleep	Sleep
1:00 am	Sleep	Sleep	Sleep	Sleep	Sleep	Sleep	Sleep
2:00 am	Sleep	Sleep	Sleep	Sleep	Sleep	Sleep	Sleep
3:00 am	Sleep	Sleep	Sleep	Sleep	Sleep	Sleep	Sleep
4:00 am	Sleep	Sleep	Sleep	Sleep	Sleep	Sleep	Sleep
5:00 am	Sleep	Sleep	Sleep	Sleep	Sleep	Sleep	Sleep
6:00 am	Sleep	Morning Routine	Morning Routine	Morning Routine	Morning Routine	Morning Routine	Sleep
7:00 am	Sleep	Commute	Commute	Commute	Commute	Commute	Sleep
8:00 am	Morning Routine	Work	Work	Work	Work	Work	Sleep
9:00 am	Morning Routine	Work	Work	Work	Work	Work	Morning Routine
10:00 am	Church	Work	Work	Work	Work	Work	Morning Routine
11:00 am	PersonalTime	Work	Work	Work	Work	Work	PersonalTime
12:00 pm	PersonalTime	Lunch	Lunch	Lunch	Lunch	Lunch	PersonalTime
1:00 pm	PersonalTime	Work	Work	Work	Work	Work	PersonalTime
2:00 pm	PersonalTime	Work	Work	Work	Work	Work	PersonalTime
3:00 pm	PersonalTime	Work	Work	Work	Work	Work	PersonalTime
4:00 pm	PersonalTime	Work	Work	Work	Work	Work	PersonalTime
5:00 pm	PersonalTime	Commute	Commute	Commute	Commute	Commute	PersonalTime
6:00 pm	PersonalTime	Dinner	Dinner	Dinner	Dinner	Dinner	PersonalTime
7:00 pm	PersonalTime	PersonalTime	PersonalTime	PersonalTime	PersonalTime	PersonalTime	PersonalTime
8:00 pm	PersonalTime	PersonalTime	PersonalTime	PersonalTime	PersonalTime	PersonalTime	PersonalTime
9:00 pm	PersonalTime	PersonalTime	PersonalTime	PersonalTime	PersonalTime	PersonalTime	PersonalTime
10:00 pm	PersonalTime	Sleep	Sleep	Sleep	Sleep	Sleep	PersonalTime
11:00 pm	Sleep	Sleep	Sleep	Sleep	Sleep	Sleep	PersonalTime

Chapter 17

Your Master Mind Miracle Team

When one door closes, another opens. But we often look so long and regretfully upon the closed door that we do not see the one which has opened for us.

Helen Keller

Remember the "Miracle on the Ice" at the 1980 Winter Olympics in New York? It was the infamous match in which the U.S. hockey team finally beat the more experienced Russians and went on to win the gold medal. A movie, released in February of 2004, told the story of how different players from around the country came together to form an Olympic gold medal team. I like this story because it eloquently portrays the power inherent in a team. And yes, it applies to your Millionaire Goal.

In the pursuit of realizing your own personal gold, you will need what I like to call your "Master Mind Team." Your team will not help you win an Olympic medal, but it will help you meet your financial goals. Remember the adage, "There is no 'I' in team"? If your goal is to have a million-dollar net worth within eight years, you will reach that goal much sooner with a team of experts behind you. It is still a million-dollar net worth whether you accomplish it with a team or on your own. Of course, if you bought this book, then you are probably already a team player.

Many Hispanic-Americans will never achieve their wealth plans simply because they look at investments, or the professionals who could help them find the investments, as an unnecessary expense. It is better to think about what your net return from the investment will be. Here is an easy example:

You net an 8 percent return with a 2 percent cost *or*

You net a 12 percent return with a 4 percent cost

It's easy to see that a 12 percent return is more than an 8 percent return, no matter what the cost to achieve it. That 4 percent cost, the cost of seeking professional advice, pays off rather nicely, doesn't it?

The following is a list of professional advisors and consultants that should be part of your Master Mind Miracle Team. You may use some or all of them. Feel free to add other professionals to your list if you find it necessary.

Internet Expert
Realtor
Financial Planner
Attorney
Tax Professional
Insurance Agent
Banker
Technology Expert
Marketing Consultant
Stock Broker/Consultant
Business Consultant
Mortgage Broker

A team of professionals can be a dynamic wealth builder for you and your family. Your team can help you "go for the gold." How do you find your team? You do it the hard way, by doing research and asking questions. You should start to accumulate a list of the ideal prospects for each category, write them in your calendar, and begin interviewing them one at a time. As you begin the selection process, you should consider their experience, their character, their reputation and integrity, their family values, what they have that their peer professionals don't, and perhaps the most important factor, whether or not you like them. It's also advisable that all of your team members like each other. Nothing will destroy a team faster than someone with an oversized ego. You don't want someone who is so wrapped up in his own profession or business that he disregards your goals and objectives or the recommendations that other team members put forth on your behalf. The questions in Chart 17-1 will help ensure that team members have the qualifications you desire.

Finally, never forget that even the nicest and most helpful people are ultimately driven by self-interest. (Hey, they're not working with you just because it's fun!) It may help to tactfully remind your team that the success of your investments and/or business is inherently linked to theirs. When you make money, they make money. Everyone wins.

Hispanic Millionaire Action Item:
Make a list of prospects for your Master Mind Team and put the names in your calendar.

Chart 17-1

Master Mind Miracle Team

Name	Phone Number	Name	Phone Number
Realtors		**Financial Planners/Advisors**	
Attorneys		**Tax Professionals**	
Insurance Agents		**Bankers**	
Technology Experts		**Marketing Consultants**	
Stock Brokers		**Business Consultants**	
Mortgage Brokers		**Internet Experts**	

Questions to Ask

1. What value-added services do you provide?
2. How do you make money for your clients?
3. What are your qualifications?
4. Why should I choose you over your competition?
5. Are you a team player?

Chapter 18

The Greatest Money Market in the World

There's nothing in the middle of the road but yellow stripes and dead armadillos.

Jim Hightower

You can be assured that the United States of America and the Free Enterprise capital system is the richest and best system in the world. Through this system the stock market has become the *money market* center for all Hispanic-Americans and the rest of the world. Through the stock market, an individual can invest as little as $50, or as much as millions of dollars, and make a return through equity or debt investing.

How can you invest in the market? There are several ways. Go to Chart 18-1(a) and look at the historical returns (past history) of market investments. Let's take each investment vehicle and learn what it can do for your investing risk tolerance. You can invest in:

Stocks
Bonds
Mutual Funds
Variable Annuities
Variable Life

Stocks:

You can pick your favorite companies, and have your advisor help you decide which ones to invest in. Individual stock inventory is probably the most misunderstood type of investment to help you become wealthy or just financially independent. When you invest in a stock, you are investing in a company, more specifically a public corporation company. In other words, the company and its records are open to the public and subject to securities regulation laws. When you invest your dollars (along with millions of other investor dollars) in ABC Corporation, you own a percentage of the company. Now what happens? What is the goal of a public company? The company is in business to make more money and profits for its shareholders You can own a piece, or a percentage, of a multi-billion-dollar company by purchasing some shares of its stock.

Whether you own one stock or an equity ownership in one corporation, you have two risks right from the start: a business risk and a market risk. The business risk is that the company itself can lose money or even go under (Enron for example). It is very rare for a public corporation to go under since it's a large business organization. After all, if it were not a profitable company, it would not have gone public to begin with. But the risk does exist.

Usually if a public company is experiencing problems or has a negative growth record, it merges with or is purchased by another public corporation. That's where the second risk, the market risk, comes in. Market risk is based on all outside factors, like inflation, taxes, interest rates, national deficits, competition, world trade, war, and so on. All these factors can decrease the share price of your stock or mutual fund, and even though this price could be for a short-term period, if you are an emotional investor you could sell and have a loss on your investment.

Is it possible to make a good or great return on individual stocks? That depends on the price at which you sell. Remember, emotions can make you sell at a loss. Owning more stocks decreases your business and market risks. There is an assumption that buying individual stocks can make you big returns overnight. While this has happened and will happen again, the determining factor is when you buy and when you sell. Usually the decision to buy is easy; the tough decision is when to sell. Most Americans don't get it.

If a stock is hot, and can produce a super three-figure return, how many investors can this happen to, and for how long of a period? The market is so perfect that if you have an overabundance of "greedy investors" the price will rise quickly. If you blink or wait one day, you will miss the so-called higher return cycle. Always remember that you are not the only one investing in the market, and even the sophisticated financial institutes that invest every day can pick occasional "dogs."

Bonds:

Bond investments are considered more conservative than stocks because there is legal obligation to pay back your principal and interest or dividends. Bonds are the only type of investment that allows you to invest with the private sector (public corporations) and the U.S. government. In other words, when you buy or invest in a bond or bond portfolio, you are lending your money to the U.S. government or to public companies. The U.S. government will pay you less interest than a public corporation because of its backing of the U.S.A. and its tax system. Government bonds are considered less risky than bonds issued through the private sector. The U.S. government can issue only bonds and other debt-type instruments (bills, notes, etc.). It cannot sell stocks. Public corporations can issue bonds and stocks. Their bond investors get paid first, before their stock (equity) investors.

The average bond returns for the last seventy-five years is about 5.5 percent for government bonds and about 6-8 percent for public corporations. For the most part, bonds pay dividends/interest every year until they mature, and then they pay you your original principal investment. The best reason to invest in bonds is that their dividends are almost always paid. The downside is that there is no growth of the bond.

So which should you invest in? Stocks offer ownership and a higher historical rate of return, due to growth and reinvestment. They have business risk and market risk. Bonds are more conservative. Since a bond is a debt, its earnings are less than stocks, and its biggest risk is inflation, or purchasing power risk. It is not necessary to invest only in stocks for your Millionaire Goal. A good asset allocation of stocks and bonds can get you to your goal. With an understanding of stocks and bonds we can explain the remaining stock market types of investments.

Mutual Funds:

A mutual fund is a portfolio containing a large number of stocks and/or bonds. Each mutual fund is managed by a team or manager whose goal is to make a profit from their selection of stocks and bonds. You can invest in a mutual fund with even a small amount of money, like $50 a month. When you invest in a mutual fund, you eliminate the business risk, since the fund has an average of about one hundred stocks and bonds (public corporations) inside the fund. You still have market risk, however. There are numerous types of mutual funds to choose from (see Chart 18-2). There is probably a mutual fund for everyone, and if you wish, you can make a portfolio of several mutual funds.

The goal of the team that manages a mutual fund is to make the highest return possible. The more return the fund makes, the more profit or bonuses the managers receive. Each shareholder of the mutual fund makes the same return based on the amount of his or her investment. So how do managers earn money for their funds? By researching and analyzing public companies and then buying the individual stocks for their funds. They also will sell those stocks that they have concluded will not be profitable. Some managers like to buy and sell often. Others like to keep some, or a majority, of the stocks in the fund for an indefinite time period. Many mutual funds have stocks and bonds in order to balance the risk tolerance.

Today in the marketplace there are more mutual funds than stocks, because of all the possible purchase combinations of stocks and bonds. Each mutual fund has a historical return and a risk tolerance (standard deviation and Sharpe Ratios).

Risk Tolerance and Management:

As I've already said, a stock represents a share of a public company and has both a business risk and a market risk. Mutual funds eliminate the business risk but still have market risk. Remember, no investment, no matter what the possible return, is right for you unless it meets your objectives and attitudes toward risk. Let's explore the components of risk management.

Systematic risk is risk that cannot be reduced any further through diversification. For example, if you own one stock, your risk is 6.6 times more than the S & P 500 (which is made up of 500 stocks/companies). But, when you own ten stocks, your risk is now only 1.6 times the S & P 500. If you owned fifty stocks, your risk would be 1.1 times.

In regard to mutual funds (an average fund has about 100-150 stocks), there are two measurements of risk that are very important to your Millionaire Goal. The first is standard deviation. Do you remember standard deviation (SD) from your business math or statistics class? One SD means 68 percent probability, two SD means 95 percent probability, and three SD means 99 percent probability. We use two standard deviations, or 95 percent probability, for our examples. In other words, a 95 percent probability means that there is a 95 percent chance that a mutual fund return or loss will end up somewhere on the bell curve, or between two points (return/loss). There is also a 2.5 percent chance that it could do better or worse.

Look at Chart 19-1, which shows a 95 percent SD bell curve probability of a fund. You can find these two stats in the prospectus of the fund or online reports of the fund. For example, a particular growth fund has a ten-year average return of 10 percent, and a standard deviation of twenty. What does this mean for its future probability? Should you invest in this fund? What is your risk tolerance? If the fund fits your risk tolerance, maybe you should invest in it.

Historical analysis is the following:

One SD = twenty, two SD = plus/minus forty (95 percent probability)

Average return = 10 percent

Our risk tolerance measurement is that there is a 95 percent probability that this fund would be between a minus thirty and a plus fifty, with an average of 10 percent, at a given future year. This is a much better way of selecting a mutual fund than, "The average return of this fund was 10 percent, and that's it." If the above risk is too much for you, find a fund with less risk, and probably less return.

The second measurement is the Sharpe Ratio. It is based on the measurement of the returns and the risk of a fund, over and above the risk-free rate of return (treasury bills), compared to the performance and risk of other funds.

In other words, it measures all growth funds with other growth funds, balance funds with balance funds, and can measure and compare different investment portfolios. The higher the Sharpe Ratio, the better the performance on a risk-adjusted basis.

When you're investing in individual stocks, there are several techniques you can use to reduce your risk. One technique is a conservative option, called Covered Calls. Once you learn this, you can stay with this option or explore others. Remember, if you take on too much, you usually end up discouraged and will not do anything to reach your Millionaire Goal.

Covered Call investing is similar to buying and selling stocks. The difference is that after you buy the stock (you own it now), you agree to sell it at a certain strike price. The right for someone else to hold or buy this agreement—to buy your shares of stock at a certain price—is known as an option. This option generates an option price or option premium, which is the key and strength of a Covered Call. Then, the option buyer pays a Covered Call writer a premium for the right, not the obligation, to buy the shares on or before the expiration date, which is the third Friday of each month. The premium is what makes Covered Call investing work over time. The sale of a Covered Call option obligates the seller, or writer, to deliver stock at the strike price of the option, if the option buyer chooses to exercise his or her option. Covered Call options can help maximize the yield of the held stock. They also minimize losses by offsetting your stock's decreased share price with additional premium income.

Hispanic Millionaire Action Item:
Start investing in the market on a monthly basis, today.

Chart 18-1(a)

Historical Market Returns

For 5, 10, 15, 20, 25 years ending 12-31-2003

	25 Years	20 Years	15 Years	10 Years	5 Years
U.S. 30-day Treasury Bill	6.1%	4.9%	4.2%	3.8%	3.0%
Dow Jones Industrial Average	10.8%	11.1%	11.0%	10.8%	2.6%
Lehman Brother Treasury Bond Index	10.1%	10.9%	9.6%	7.7%	6.0%
Lehman Long-Term Credit Bond Index	10.4%	11.0%	9.7%	8.1%	7.4%
MSCI-EAFE Equity Index	10.9%	11.1%	4.0%	4.8%	0.3%
NAREIT REIT	13.0%	10.3%	11.2%	13.0%	16.7%
NASDAQ	13.1%	11.2%	12.4%	10.3	(-1.8%)
Russell 2000 Growth Index	10.3%	6.9%	7.9%	5.5%	0.9%
Russell 2000 Value Index	15.8%	12.9%	13.3%	12.7%	12.3%
S & P 500	10.3%	10.0%	9.7%	9.0%	(-2.06%)
Portfolio: 10% of Each Index Above	11.7%	10.4%	9.9%	9.0%	5.2%

Chart 18-1(b)

Historical Market Indexes

U.S. 30-day Treasury Bill an index based upon the average monthly yield of 30-day Treasury Bills.
Dow Jones Industrial Average an unmanaged price weighted index of 30 of the largest, most widely held stocks.
Lehman Brother Treasury Bond Index a total return index of all public organizations of the U.S. Treasury.
Lehman Long-Term Credit Bond Index a total return index of all publicly issued, fixed-rate, non-convertible, investment-grade domestic corporate bonds.
MSCI-EAFE Equity Index a total return index in U.S. dollars based or share prices and reinvested gross dividends of approximately 1,100 companies from 20 countries (Europe & Far East).
NAREIT REIT National Association of Real Estate Investment Trust total return to include all REIT trading on NYSE, and includes real estate investments.
NASDAQ an index of 3,000 OTC issues with an aggregate market value of approximately $500 billion, made up of domestic common stocks.
Russell 2000 Growth Index stocks are selected from 2,000 small companies with higher price-to-book ratios and higher forecasted growth values.
Russell 2000 Value Index stocks are selected from 2,000 small companies and with lower price-to-book ratios and lower forecasted growth values.
S & P 500 an unmanaged market capitalization weighted price index of 500 widely held common stocks listed on the NYSE, AMEX, and OTC market.
Portfolio made up of 10 percent of each of the 10 indexes in chart 18-1(a).

Chart 18-2

Types of Mutual Funds Based on Investment Objective

Asset Allocation Funds that offer diversification within asset classes and among different asset classes; usually are made up of stocks, bonds, and money market investments.

Balanced Funds Diversified investments between stocks and bonds; their primary objectives are preservation of capital and moderate growth of income and principal.

Bond Funds A wide variety of portfolio bond types.

Growth Funds Funds that concentrate on long-term capital gains and future income, usually no current income; majority in common stocks.

Hedge Funds Aggressive techniques to include short sales, use of puts and calls, high leverage, for maximum growth.

Income Funds Invest in securities that usually pay above current rates of return from either dividends or interest; usually a majority of fund portfolio is invested in bonds.

Index Funds Funds that try to match performance of some market index by creating a portfolio that is similar, to try to outperform the market on a risk-adjusted basis.

International Funds Invest in stocks or bonds of companies that are foreign and have many types, depending on countries and industries.

Money Market Funds Invest in T-Bills, CDs, and corporate commercial paper, providing current income and relative safety of principal.

Sector Funds Investments to particular sectors in the market, like health care or chemicals, etc.

Specialty Funds Investments in a single industry, a group of related industries, defined geographical region, or non-security assets.

Tax Exempt Funds Investments in municipal bonds or other securities that offer tax sheltered income.

Chapter 19

The Greatest Money Market Part II

I cannot give you the formula for success, but I can give you the formula for failure: try to please everybody.

Herbert Bayard Swope

Now that you have a good understanding of how stocks and mutual funds work, we can proceed to cover additional investments in the market. The next two types of investments are called variables. The first is variable annuities, and the second is variable life. These two types of investments have the unique characteristic of encompassing two industries—insurance and securities—in their final products. This combination results in some additional benefits: tax-advantaged investment, guarantees, exchanges, creditor protection (not all states), and a death benefit. Inside each of the two investment vehicles are mutual fund accounts, or investment sub-accounts as they are called. Let's look at both vehicles.

<u>Variable Annuities:</u>

A variable annuity is a combination of insurance companies' benefits and mutual fund companies' benefits. Its greatest advantage is that no taxes are due on any earnings until you withdraw from the annuity plan. When you withdraw any of your monies, earnings come out before principal and are taxable. If you withdraw before age fifty-nine-and-a-half, there is an additional 10 percent tax penalty. There is also a way to take out earnings from your variable annuity and pay taxes on the earnings, but not suffer the 10 percent penalty. It is done through Section 72 of the IRS code. You can "temporarily annuitize" your investment account and receive the income for the greater of a) five years or b) the number of years until you reach age fifty-nine-and-a-half. After the longer time period, you can revert to your variable annuity market value account. There are no loan provisions for variable annuities, but there are loan provisions for some qualified retirement plans with variable annuities as their product or investment.

Variable annuities usually contain a guaranteed death benefit on the original investment or contribution. This means that even if the market value of your sub-account is down 50 percent, the death benefit is at least 100 percent of the original investment. Another benefit of variable annuities is that there is no limit to the amount of contribution or investment you can make. Most states provide complete or partial protection from creditors to variable annuities.

Many new benefits have been added to variable annuities that were not available ten, or even five, years ago. Many variable annuities offer living benefits. The living benefits have two major benefits. The benefits are like a combination of a defined contribution plan (such as IRAs and 401(k)s) and a defined benefit plan (such as a lifetime pension or Social Security). You can choose which one to use depending on the market and on your objectives. With this plan, you always have access to your defined contribution plan, or lump sum of the market value of your account. If the United States experiences a down market during your retirement years, you can convert your variable annuity into a defined benefit plan, where you will receive a guaranteed monthly income check for life. There are not many investment plans or retirement plans that give you two options for investments or retirement.

Speaking of monthly income checks, many Hispanic-Americans have a perception that a variable annuity, or any annuity for that matter, is a lifetime monthly check (annuitization) on which you have no more principal, or no more control of your investment principal. That is not true. If you want to annuitize a CD or a mutual fund, you have the option. If you decide to annuitize a lump sum amount of money, you are rewarded by receiving part principal (which is not taxable) and part earnings (which is taxable), for the rest of your life. You also can have a variable annuity and control the principal for the rest of your life by making systematic withdrawals. Another benefit of variable and fixed annuities is a 1035 Tax-Free Exchange for another annuity. This is similar to the rollover or transfer options for qualified retirement plans.

The variable annuity of today, with its living income benefits, step-up market value, and guarantees, is an extremely attractive investment for retirement. Most of the major benefits of variable annuities came about around 1997-1998. If you own a fixed or variable annuity because of the 1035 Tax-Free Exchange Programs granted by the IRS, you should review any annuities and compare.

Variable Life:

This investment is a unique and often misunderstood investment plan. What is variable life? The short explanation is that it is a way for you to contribute a certain amount of money that is then invested in mutual-fund-type sub-accounts. Those funds pay for the life insurance cost from the investment sub-accounts.

The earnings from the sub-accounts grow tax-free, and the investment account pays for the cost of life insurance tax-free as well. It has a loan provision that allows you to borrow a non-taxable amount from earnings. The variable life investment can out-perform an investment plan with term life insurance and an alternate investment. Why is this? The answer is that the inside earnings of the variable life policy are tax-free, and from those tax-free earnings, it pays for the "term" life insurance cost. Outside of variable life, your term life premium is paid for with after-tax dollars.

If you plan carefully with your savings, you can literally turn your variable life investment into a "private bank" and can use it to pay for automobiles, homes, college education, debts, and create a retirement income stream that is tax-free. (You might compare it to a Roth IRA with no contribution limits and no income qualification.) You may have to look at several hypothetical illustrations to see exactly what variable life can do for you. Variable life pays a death benefit to your family that is, again, tax-free. This is the only investment that I know of with equity-type investments that can be made income tax-free whether you are living or dead.

Real Estate Investment Trusts (REITs):

REITs are investments that can be invested in many types of real estate, without the headache of maintenance or collecting rents. A REIT enables small investors to make investments in professionally-managed, large, institutional-quality, commercial real estate. In general, a REIT has to pay dividends to investors of at least 90 percent of its taxable income for each year. REITs avoid the federal "double taxation" treatment of income that generally results from investments in a corporation. REITs have had an attractive average return of 12.5 percent from 1972-2001. By diversifying your investment portfolio of stocks, bonds, and cash, REITs provide a decreased risk tolerance and increased return.

Your Optimum Portfolio:

When a person decides to put money away for the long-term, he or she soon realizes that there is an optimum portfolio available for everyone. The optimum portfolio is based on returns and risk tolerance. Whether you are conservative, moderate, or aggressive, there is an optimum portfolio for you. What is your risk tolerance? Do you know what your current or future portfolio looks like? There could be a hundred different asset allocation portfolio combinations, but in the investment industry most providers show, or illustrate, four major ones. The other portfolio combinations are made up of these four. Each portfolio has a standard deviation and average return based on past records. See Chart 19-1 for the four portfolios and their 95 percent standard deviation probability projection:

Principal-Conservative——————Average return is 4 percent, probability of future return to fall between +2 percent and +6 percent.

Conservative————————Average return is 8 percent, probability of future return to fall between -8 percent and +24 percent.

Moderate—————————Average return is 11 percent, probability of future return to fall between -15 percent and +37 percent.

Aggressive————————Average return is 13 percent, probability of future return to fall between -26 percent and + 52 percent.

There is also a chance for a 2.5 percent greater return and a 2.5 percent greater loss.

Where does your portfolio fit today, and where do you want it to be tomorrow?

Go to the optimum portfolio chart (Chart 19-2). Your portfolio will be somewhere on this chart. If you think back to an earlier chapter, you will remember that the vertical axis (top to bottom) is the "return" line, and the horizontal axis (left to right) is the "risk" or "standard deviation" line. The farther to the right of the graph, the greater the risk becomes, the further up the graph, the higher the return. With education and professional advice you can create an optimum portfolio.

Hispanic Millionaire Action Item:
There is not one investment that is immune to risk. Diversify your total portfolio for the long run.

Chart 19-1

Standard Deviation – (2)

95% Probability

Portfolios

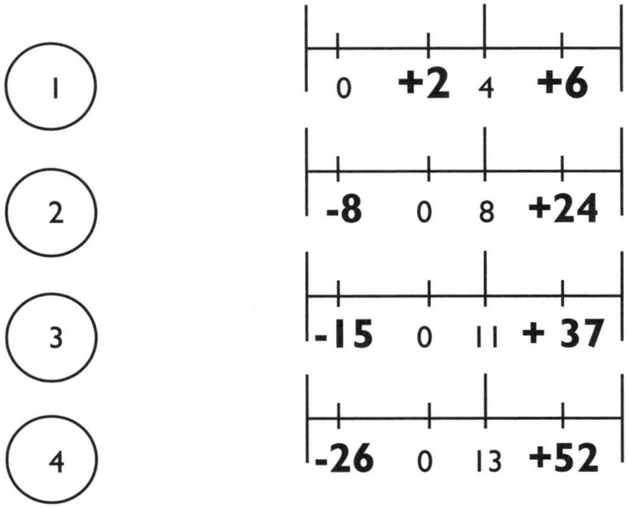

What range of risk are you comfortable with?

Chart 19-2

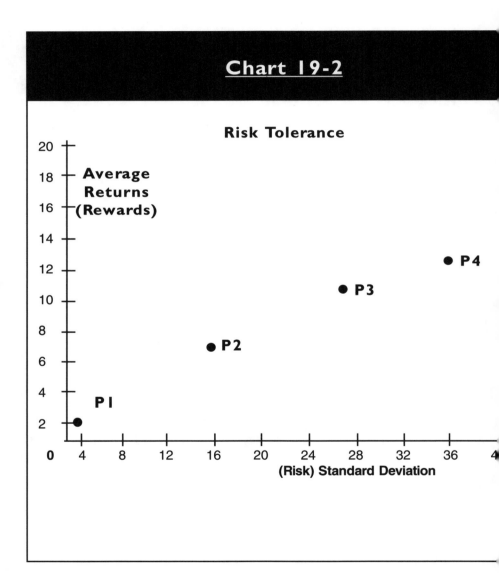

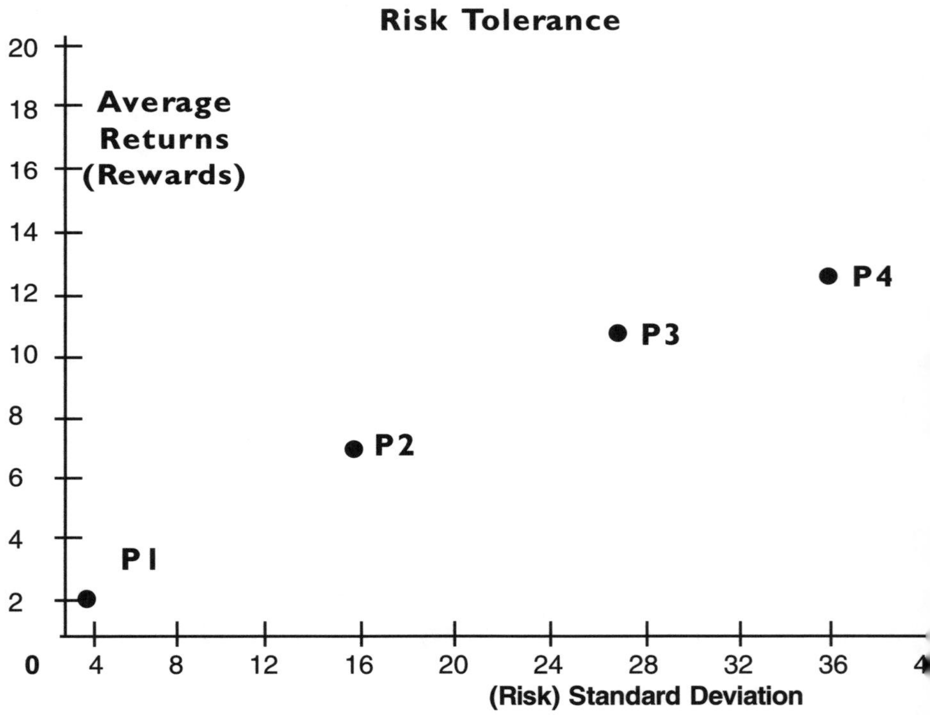
Risk Tolerance
Average Returns (Rewards)
20
18
16
14
12
10
8
6
4
2
0
4
8
12
16
20
24
28
32
36
P1
P2
P3
P4
(Risk) Standard Deviation

Chapter 20

Make the IRS Your Partner, Not Your Enemy

What isn't tried won't work.

Claude McDonald

Most Hispanic-Americans have not taken advantage of all the great laws that our President and Congress have made for our benefit. As Will Rogers said, "I am very willing to pay my taxes to my country, but I would be very happy to pay half of the taxes." You have the right as a Hispanic-American to take advantage of every type of IRS tax deduction and tax break. But you will have to take action; the IRS cannot tell you what you can or cannot do.

When I say to "make the IRS your partner," I am saying that if you pay taxes on investments, it is because you want to pay taxes. You can make the IRS your partner in several stages of your investment: on the contribution of your invested capital, on the earnings from those investments, and on the withdrawal of the earnings and principal in the future. You should take advantage of every type of IRS-approved investment that has any of the following characteristics or benefits:

* Tax-Deduction * Tax-Deferred * Tax-Free * Tax-Advantaged

I will start at the beginning to help you determine which, if any, of the tax-advantaged investments you can qualify for and implement in your own financial planning. The first investment involves saving a certain amount of money each month or even each year without paying taxes on that contribution. Suppose, for example, that you are in the 30 percent tax bracket, and you make a contribution of $2,000 to an investment plan that doesn't come with a tax break. You actually have to earn $2,857: $857 to pay in taxes to the IRS, and $2,000 for your investment. With an IRS tax deduction, you will save the $857 in taxes. This means you have an additional $857 to invest before taxes.

How can the IRS become your partner in your wealth and/or retirement plan? Do you remember the Rule of Seventy-two? Take any interest/earnings rate and divide it into seventy-two and you get the number of years it will take to double your money. Use the Rule to determine the number of years for $2,857 and $2,000. Many of you may be taking advantage of the first investment type already in the form of a 401(k) or 403(b) plan or an IRA. If you are fortunate enough to work for an employer who matches your contribution, you now have an investment/retirement plan that includes you and two partners: your employer and the IRS. This is a triple whammy that will help you in the process of accumulating wealth.

Here is an example of how such plans work: Mario Vasquez works for "SOSA Digital, Inc." The company matches an employee's contributions to up to 6 percent of his or her salary. (Company match can be anywhere from 1 to 6 percent.) Mario makes $47,616 a year. Originally, Mario believed that he would have to "pay" to invest in his company's retirement plan. But after reading this book, Mario understands future goal planning and wealth accumulation, and he maximizes his contribution of 6 percent. Let's look at what he did with his money:

$47,616 salary x 6% =	$2,857	Employer
$47,616 salary x 6% =	$2,857	Employee (Mario)
IRS tax bracket—30% =	$ 857	Tax Savings
Total Contributions =	$5,714	Mario's Retirement

Total NET Out-of-Pocket for Mario = $2,000

Now, you tell me who will accumulate more wealth and enjoy a more prosperous retirement, the person who invests $2,000 a year, or the person who invests $5,714 a year? Compare each investment using your Rule of Seventy-two for each year, or go to Chart 5-1 to compare annually.

If you work for an employer who matches your retirement funds and you have not taken full advantage of this benefit, then you are throwing your money away. Please go to your employer and increase your contribution ASAP. By the way, if your employer has a 401(k) or similar retirement plan, you as an employee should be able to contribute more than 6 percent a year.

If you work for an educational organization, a public or private school system, or a non-profit organization, you are eligible to contribute up to $14,000 before taxes in 2005 through a 403(b) retirement plan. If you work for an employer who doesn't offer a qualified retirement plan, take him or her out to lunch and ask if the company could set one up. Even if your employer does not match your contributions, you can still enjoy tremendous tax breaks. Perhaps you will be able to talk him or her into matching at a later lunch. You would be surprised at the number of employers who set up matching retirement plans because their employees ask for it, or better yet, organize it. Cost to the company is minimal, and besides, most employers realize that the more benefits they offer, the more loyal and hardworking employees will be. It is much more cost effective for employers to set up a qualified retirement tax plan than to lose employees to other companies.

If you have no employer-sponsored plan and can't convince your boss to implement one, then you are eligible for an IRA. In 2004, the maximum amount that could be contributed was $3,000. The amount will increase to $4,000 from 2005 to 2007, and increase again to $5,000 in 2008. After 2008 the maximum contribution amount will increase according to the cost of living adjustment (COLA). There is also a "catch-up" provision for those who are fifty years of age or more. The provision increases the annual contribution limits so that you can "catch up" on the amount of money that you will have for retirement if you didn't begin contributing as early as you would have liked (See Chart 20-1). You get the same tax benefits as your employer's plan, but not until you file your 1040.

The next type of IRS partner plan is one in which only your earnings are tax-deferred, while your contribution is still taxable. For example, if Jorge Cruz has maxed out his employer plan or his IRA, what are his other options? There are two great options, and many millionaires have money invested in both: tax-deferred annuities and tax-deferred life insurance plans. Let's review each: tax-deferred annuities offer the option of investing or contributing funds to an investment product where there is no maximum contribution amount and all of the earnings grow tax-deferred. We get the same tax-deferred earnings available in the first plan, but there is no tax break on the contribution. However, if we compared both plans, and the investment return was the same, we would have the same accumulation.

Example: Jorge is able to put away $10,000 into an annuity that earns 10 percent, or $1,000. If Jorge is in the 30 percent tax bracket, the IRS is his partner for $300, which means that $700 comes from Jorge's earnings. You compound your earnings with a tax-deferred accumulation of $1,000. Next year the earnings will be 10 percent of $11,000, tax-deferred, and the process will repeat itself every year you have the investment annuity. If you invested outside an annuity or tax-qualified retirement plan, you would pay IRS federal income taxes on the invested contribution and/or the earnings. The IRS gives you a tax break so that you can accumulate money for your retirement years, but if you happen to retire early and want to withdraw the funds before the age of 59.5, you will have to pay a 10 percent penalty. The difference between the plans is that there is a 10 percent penalty on 100 percent of your tax-qualified plan (contributions and earnings), but the penalty applies only on the earnings part of the tax-deferred annuity.

Most states have laws that protect retirement plans and tax-deferred accounts from creditors. Many millionaire investors want to have the creditor-proof benefit first, over their tax-deferred earnings return benefit. The other tax-deferred product is life insurance polices. Life insurance policies have many benefits, options, and uses. There are entire books on the topic of life insurance. I will briefly discuss the tax and investment benefits of life insurance policies in this chapter.

In a nutshell, you contribute a certain savings amount, yearly or monthly, and earnings are credited to your account. As a result, all insurance costs and expenses are paid from this account. The earnings from the investment options (there are many) grow tax-deferred or tax-free. One of the benefits often overlooked is that the cost of insurance is paid out of the tax-deferred investment account. That means the IRS pays your insurance costs with earnings that are not taxed. In the long-term it can be substantially cheaper than the best term insurance rates.

Another great benefit of life insurance policies is that you can take out a loan on your cash value, with a low or even zero interest rate, and use it to get out of debt. You won't have any taxes due on the loan or withdrawal. Most Hispanic-Americans don't realize that they can actually create a life insurance plan that offers substantial cash and retirement benefits that can be withdrawn tax-free.

The third type of tax plan is the capital gains tax. The tax law of 2002 reduced the capital gains tax. If you hold an investment twelve months or more and sell it for a profit, your long-term capital gains tax is 15 percent for individuals who are in a 25 percent or higher tax bracket. If you are in a 15 percent tax bracket or lower, the capital gains tax maximum is 5 percent. Common investments for capital gains taxes are stocks, mutual funds, real estate, and business equity.

The fourth type of tax-advantaged investment is one that is tax-free. There are three major products: municipal bonds, life insurance, and Roth IRAs. Municipal bonds are tax-free because they are invested in government or municipal types of lending—for example, to cities, schools, counties, and state governments. The earnings from the investment are tax-free. Roth IRAs, if you remember, have the same maximum contribution as traditional IRAs. The difference, besides the tax-free earnings, is the adjusted gross income of the taxpayer. If you have a pension plan, it can disqualify you from being able to purchase an IRA. Life insurance contributors have no maximum, provided they qualify for the insurance death benefit. Their contributions are not affected by adjusted gross income.

As I said earlier, you can set up a withdrawal income benefit for an indefinite period of time tax-free. And upon your death, the insurance proceeds go to your beneficiary income tax-free.

I did not discuss federal estate taxes in this chapter. They will be outlined in a later chapter. Based on the current general consensus in Washington, estate taxes will require a very high net worth, or will be taxed differently in the future than they are today. In any case, an estate tax problem is a good problem to have. It means you are a millionaire, and that is the goal, is it not?

Hispanic Millionaire Action Item:
Take care of every tax-advantaged plan you are eligible for this year.

Chart 20-1

Retirement Plan Pre-Tax Contributions

Maximum Limits *

	2004	2005
IRAs Plans		
Annually	$ 3,000	$ 4,000
Catch-up	$ 500	$ 500
401(k), 403(b), 457 Plans		
Annually	$13,000	$14,000
Catch-up	$ 3,000	$ 4,000
Simple Plan		
Annually	$ 9,000	$10,000
Catch-up	$ 1,500	$ 2,000
Defined Contribution Plan	$41,000	$42,000
Defined Benefit Plan	$165,000	$170,000

* Subject to change with tax acts or laws

Chapter 21

Make a Million Dollars on Your Own Homes

There are three types of baseball players: those who make it happen, those who watch it happen, and those who wonder what happened.

Tommy Lasorda

How many houses does the average Hispanic-American buy in his or her lifetime? It can be three or more. Usually a couple's first home is a small starter home. After they have children, they buy a bigger one. Then they might buy or even build a bigger dream home. For many, that third house will be the one they live in for the rest of their lives. Others may decide to sell that house at retirement in order to buy a smaller, more manageable home. The way Hispanic-Americans buy homes could change drastically in the near future. Instead of buying one to three homes in their lifetime, they might buy six to ten homes. Why? Because their Millionaire Goal, along with a new tax law established in 2002, will give them the incentive to invest in real estate, not just buy it. The Home Investment Exemption Law gave Americans a new home equity tax exemption in 2002. The law states:

1. When you sell your home and make a profit, there is no required time period in which you must buy another home.
2. The Home Investment Exemption maximum is $250,000 for single individuals and $500,000 for married couples (filing a joint tax return).

In other words, you can make up to $500,000 tax-free. That's a half-million dollars to invest wherever you want. (Not bad, huh?) You do pay taxes on any earnings that result from your investment—whether they are due currently or deferred until retirement—but the original $500,000 principal is not taxed. However, there are some restrictions. In order to claim the exemption of up to $500,000, there are two prerequisites you must meet. During the five-year period ending on the date of the sale of your home you must have:

1. Owned the home for at least two years, and
2. Used the home as your main live-in residence for at least two years.

You can maximize your tax-free exemption for your wealth and Millionaire Goal if you do the following:

1. Make a profit on the sale of your home.
2. Move every two to five years.
3. Meet the ownership and usage requirements.
4. Rent the home for up to three years after you move, if needed.
5. Buy and sell your homes until the maximum $500,000 is reached.

After you reach the tax-free $500,000 maximum, any additional profit is subject to the capital gains rate, which is currently 15 percent. Not bad.

How many homes must you live in and sell at a profit in order to reach the $500,000 maximum (or $250,000 if you are single)? It depends on the market in your area, and whether it is a buyer's or a seller's market for each home sale. The national average for appreciated residential real estate has been about 6 percent annually. Some market areas have appreciated 10 percent annually. The time that you choose to sell may not be a good one for a profit, so renting your home for up to three years may be a great option. (Of course, this depends on the rental market in your area.) You have to work hard for your home equity profit. Your real estate team member can be the key to the successful buying and selling of your homes.

If you look at Chart 21-1, you will see a hypothetical example of what the average couple can do to maximize their $500,000 tax-free exemption by selling their old home and buying a new one every four years. Buying a new home can become a fun and challenging experience, instead of a terrible chore. The projected amounts show no rental income, a 5 percent down payment on the new home (buying), a 6 percent appreciation annually, and a net selling price after expenses. It does not show closing expenses for buyers, which may be offset on their tax returns. Buying a new home every four years requires a lot of work in order to create equity. It's up to you and your real estate team to negotiate the buying and selling of your homes. It can work out very profitably for you if you do your homework.

Chart 21-2 shows what will happen if you take your home equity net profit and invest it at a hypothetical 10 percent return using forty years as your goal. In year four you should have a profit, or investment money, for the next thirty-six years (forty minus four years). If you were to invest the profit from each home sale, at year forty (add your current age to it), you and your spouse would have an accumulated return of over $3 million. Who says you can't become a millionaire by buying a new home?

Hispanic Millionaire Action Item:
Take time this month to write out your home buying and selling goal sheets.

Chart 21-1

Tax-Free Home Exemption

Hypothetical Goal

Homes	Year	Buy	Sell	Home Exemption
Home 1	1 yr	$80,000		
	4 yrs		$100,000	$20,000
Home 2	4 yrs	$120,000		
	8 yrs		$150,000	$30,000
Home 3	8 yrs	$190,000		
	12 yrs		$240,000	$50,000
Home 4	12 yrs	$280,000		
	16 yrs		$350,000	$70,000
Home 5	16 yrs	$380,000		
	20 yrs		$475,000	$95,000
Home 6	20 yrs	$500,000		
	24 yrs		$630,000	$130,000
Home 7	24 yrs	$650,000		
	28 yrs		$755,000	$105,000
Home 8	28 yrs	$450,000		
		Retire		
Totals		**$2,650,000**	**$2,700,000**	**$500,000**

Chart 21-2

Home Exemption Investment

40-Year Wealth Goal

Years	Investment Amount	Number of Years Invested	Year 40 @ 8%	Year 40 @ 10%
4 yrs	$20,000	36 yrs	$319,000	$618,000
8 yrs	$30,000	32 yrs	$351,000	$633,000
12 yrs	$50,000	28 yrs	$431,000	$721,000
16 yrs	$70,000	24 yrs	$443,000	$688,000
20 yrs	$95,000	20 yrs	$442,000	$638,000
24 yrs	$130,000	16 yrs	$444,000	$596,000
28 yrs	$105,000	12 yrs	$263,000	$328,000
Total Home Exemption Wealth Accumulation			$2,693,000	$4,222,000

Chart 21-3

Home Tax-Free Exemption Wealth Goal

Home Number	Year	Buy	Sell	Home Exemption $

Chapter 22

Real Estate Profits

It takes as much courage to have tried and failed,
as it does to have tried and succeeded.
Anne Morrow Lindbergh

There are many ways to make a profit in real estate. I will touch on several of them in this chapter. The first way, of course, is the traditional one: buying a house to live in for a while, then selling it and buying another one, and so forth. The second is to purchase investment property and either receive positive monthly cash flow or allow property to appreciate in value. The third type of real estate investment is known as *flipping*. The fourth type is an REIT investment, which I will cover shortly. For now, however, let's talk about flipping.

The goal here is to buy a real estate property and sell it within a short period of time—anywhere from one to twelve months after the purchase. Sometimes you even sell it before your original closing is finalized. Why would you buy property that you want to sell as soon as possible? Because while you are in the buying and selling process, you might find an enthusiastic tenant who will buy the property from you at a higher price and the right terms. (Actually, it does not matter if you have a tenant or not, as long as there is a buyer; however, having a tenant could add to the speed of the sale.) You may also decide to make the "flip" property a "buy and hold" property because of its excellent positive cash flow.

None of this is as easy as it sounds. The trick is to buy either a) a great property, or b) a not-so-great property that you get on your own terms. Many Hispanic-Americans lose money or have a negative cash flow because they invest in real estate based on the seller's terms. Who says you can't offer the seller the terms *you* want? It doesn't mean the seller will accept them, but that's the point of the negotiation process. You might make twenty offers before the seller accepts. So what? This one property could make you a significant profit, right?

If you want the seller to accept your first offer, then go ahead and offer the selling price of the property. If you were to do this on several properties, you might want to have some liquid funds available to make the mortgage payments. It's always that first contract that pushes the majority of Hispanic-Americans out of the real estate business. Once you have made an offer, you want to be certain that your contract gives you a way out in case you uncover some costly details about the property that you are unable to finance. Your Master Mind team members should help you here. As we said earlier, the trick is to buy the right type of real estate. In other words, you buy at the lowest price possible, or 20 percent below market value. You may not be able to buy a great property from a seller who is like you and is looking to maximize his or her profit. In that case you should look for properties that have some problems that you can fix or have some emotional issues attached that can be used to your advantage during negotiations.

Examples of Flipping a Property for a Great Return

1. Buy a property at $60,000 that is later appraised at $80,000. You or your realtor find a buyer in the $70,000-80,000 range.

2. Buy a property for $150,000 that is appraised at $180,000. You get a note for $150,000 at 6 percent and sell for $180,000 at $3,000 down and carry a note for $177,000 at 7.25 percent.
3. Buy a property for $100,000 that is appraised at $120,000. Your expenses are $1,000 a month, you get $1,200 a month in rental income, and then sell in two to ten years, depending on the appreciation and cash flow return.

A fourth way of investing in real estate is through real estate investment trusts (REITs). You are actually buying shares of several commercial real estate properties across the United States. You could own a piece of a great hotel, office building, warehouse, shopping center, or resort—all in one investment package, and at a minimum of about $5,000. There are two types of REITs: those that leverage investment capital with financing of the real estate properties, and those that have no financing. The more assets you own, the more diversified you are toward your long-term rate of return and risk tolerance.

Real estate is an area of investing that can have ups and downs, depending on the different markets you work within. Historically, real estate has averaged about 6 percent appreciation for average markets. It can be much higher in areas where the economy is booming. It can also cost you if the economy busts due to overdevelopment.

You now know four ways to invest in real estate. Each is an effective way to help you become a millionaire. You can own real estate in the following ways: (1) investing in your own homes, (2) buying and holding property, (3) flipping properties, and (4) REITs. Once you have mastered these options, you can try other real estate investments, such as raw land and commercial properties. When you find one you like, you can do it over and over again, and watch your profits add up.

Hispanic Millionaire Action Item:
Start looking at real estate properties and
write a contract offer.

Chart 22-1

Real Estate Mortgage Rates & Terms

$100,000 Loan*

	5%	6%	7%	**ARM or Interest Only @ 4.5%
30-year payment	$537	$600	$665	$375
Balance in 5 years	$91,800	$93,000	$94,000	$100,000
15-year payment	$790	$844	$900	$375
Balance in 5 years	$74,500	$76,000	$77,000	$100,000
Total payments — 30 years	$193,256	$215,838	$239,510	X
Total payments —15 years	$142,343	$151,894	$161,788	X

* Includes Principal and Interest
** Interest Only Mortgages can change monthly or annually or after 3-5 years.

Chart 22-2

Real Estate Mortgage Rates & Terms

Your Loan__________*

	5%	7%	?%	**ARM or Interest Only @ ?%
30-year payment				
Balance in 5 years				
15-year payment				
Balance in 5 years				
Total payments — 30 years				X
Total payments —15 years				X

* Includes Principal and Interest
** Interest Only Mortgages can change monthly or annually or after 3-5 years.

Chart 22-3

Investing Mortgage Payments
$100,000 Loan @ 6%
30-Year Payment $600 15-Year Payment $844

Invest Difference $244*

Years to Invest	8%	10%	12%
5 Years	$18,534	$19,646	$20,818
10 Years	$45,794	$51,328	$57,535
15 Years	$85,849	$102,304	$122,244
20 Years	$144,702	$184,464	$236,260
25 Years	$231,166	$316,751	$437,238
30 Years	$358,211	$529,792	$791,409

*You can also compare an interest only loan with any 15-year or 30-year conventional loan.

Chapter 23

Your Income Model Plan

Small opportunities are often the beginning of great enterprises.

Demosthenes

What does your income model look like at present? Do you even know? It may look like this:

Income Received .... 100 percent

Expenses .... 103 percent

Net loss .... -3 percent

Have you ever been told to save whatever money is left over after you pay all of your bills and other monthly expenses? This type of "savings" is self-defeating; it rarely ever works. You have to save first and then pay your expenses from the balance, which becomes your "new" 100 percent. This can be somewhat difficult if you have debt and your lifestyle requires the use of your entire income. But if your goal is to become a millionaire, you're just going to have to change your lifestyle. And that means you have to start thinking like a millionaire.

Begin with a percentage goal for savings and investments every month. You can then increase your savings goal monthly, quarterly, semi-annually, or annually. Your income model may not look like you thought. Remember, however, that when your goal is to become a millionaire, and you have never done any of this before, planning an income model can be very daunting. Don't worry. I will cover several income models in this chapter. Your first, second, or even your third income model may not look exactly like the sample models, but with financial practice they will.

Let's identify the key terms of your income model:

LE	=	Living Expenses
SI	=	Savings/Investments
TX	=	Taxes
IE	=	Investment Education
DT	=	Debt
CT	=	Charity/Tithe

All models are based on a 100 percent use of your personal or family income.

<u>INCOME MODEL 1:</u>

LE	80%		
TX	20%		
DT	3%	=	103%

<u>INCOME MODEL 2:</u>

LE	50%		
TX	20%		
DT	10%		
SI	10%		
IE	10%	=	100%

INCOME MODEL 3:

LE	60%		
TX	20%		
DT	10%		
SI	10%	=	100%

INCOME MODEL 4:

LE	50%		
TX	20%		
SI	20%		
IE	10%	=	100%

INCOME MODEL 5:

LE	45%		
TX	20%		
SI	20%		
IE	10%		
CT	5%	=	100%

INCOME MODEL 6:

LE	35%		
TX	20%		
SI	20%		
IE	20%		
CT	5%	=	100%

INCOME MODEL 7:

LE	35%		
TX	20%		
SI	25%		
IE	10%		
CT	10%	=	100%

INCOME MODEL 8:

LE	35%		
TX	20%		
SI	30%		
IE	5%		
CT	10%	=	100%

INCOME MODEL 9:

LE	25%		
TX	20%		
SI	30%		
IE	15%		
CT	10%	=	100%

INCOME MODEL 10:

LE	25%		
TX	30%		
SI	20%		
IE	15%		
CT	10%	=	100%

Your personal/family income models will probably not match the sample models exactly. Everyone has a different income when they start working toward their Millionaire Goal, and their debt, savings, taxes, education investment, and tithes will also be different. Your most important goal should be to allocate your total income (100 percent) to each part of the model as a percentage of your total income. You might do only 1-3 percent of your income for each of your income allocation goals. You should have a good working knowledge of your cash flow when you set up your current and future income models.

You should project at least six models over the next ten to twenty years, depending on your Millionaire Goal timeline. You will need to write down a model for each year in order to achieve your income model goals. Remember, you can always adjust later.

Hispanic Millionaire Action Item:
Create your first income model this month,
and your future ones within the year.

Chart 23-1

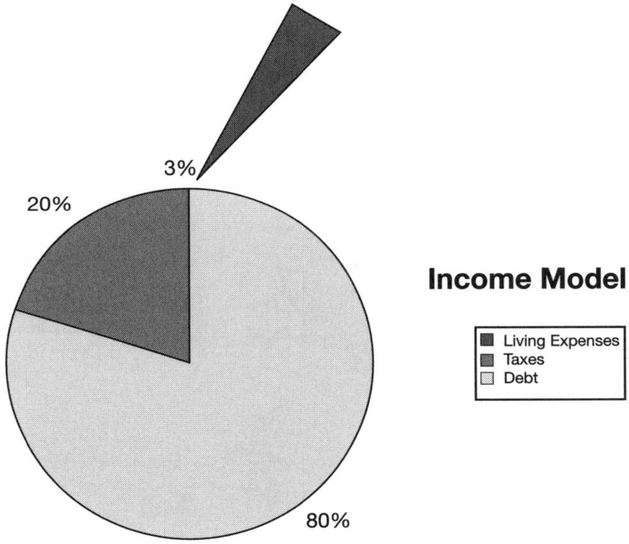
3%
20%
80%
Income Model 1
Living Expenses
Taxes
Debt

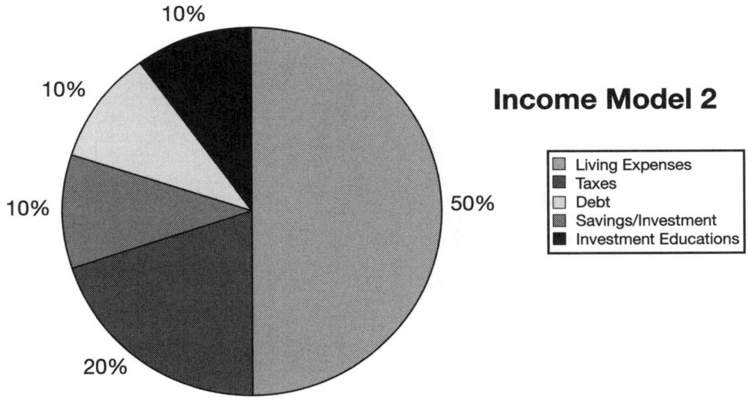
10%
10%
10%
50%
20%
Income Model 2
Living Expenses
Taxes
Debt
Savings/Investment
Investment Educations

Chart 23-1

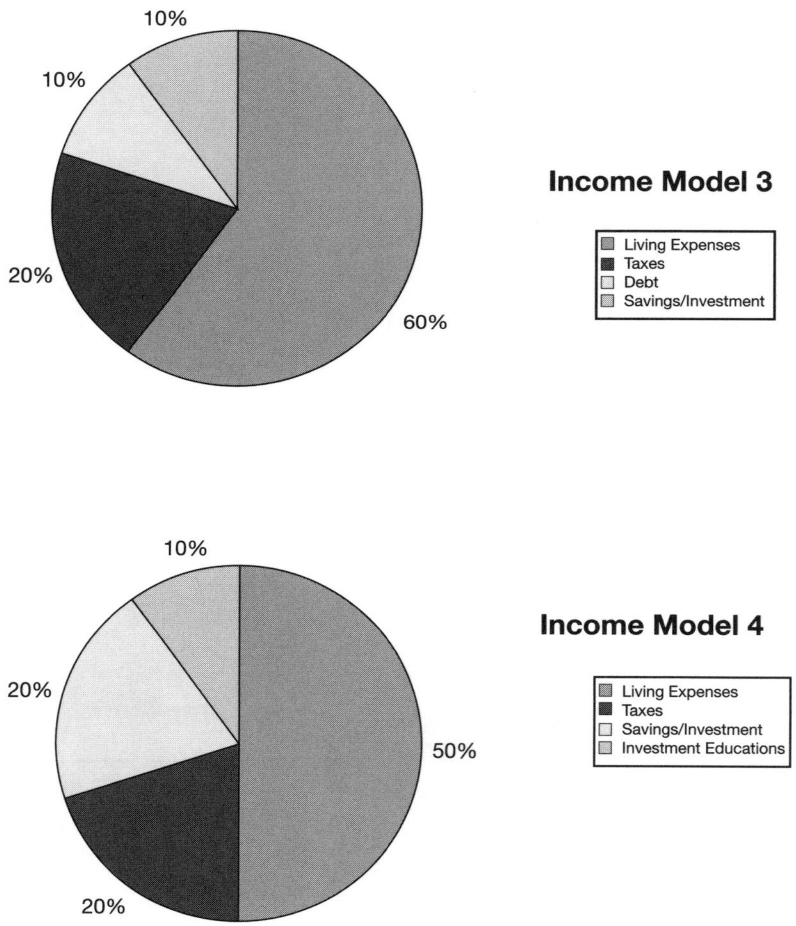
10%
10%
20%
60%
Income Model 3
Living Expenses
Taxes
Debt
Savings/Investment
10%
20%
20%
50%
Income Model 4
Living Expenses
Taxes
Savings/Investment
Investment Educations

Chart 23-1

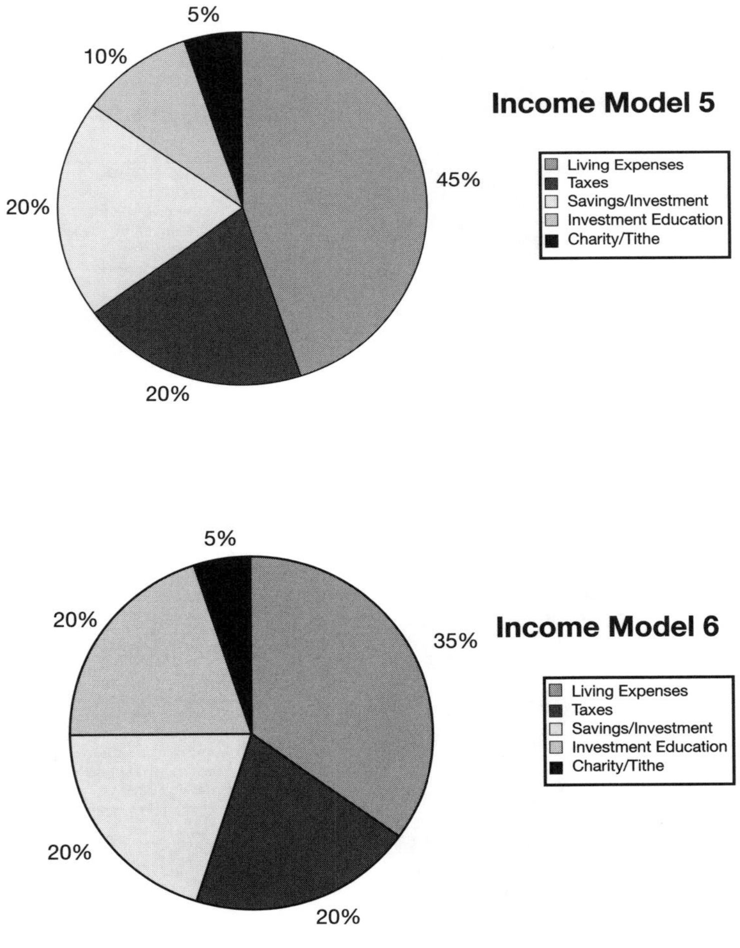
Income Model 5
5%
10%
45%
20%
20%
Living Expenses
Taxes
Savings/Investment
Investment Education
Charity/Tithe
Income Model 6
5%
20%
35%
20%
20%
Living Expenses
Taxes
Savings/Investment
Investment Education
Charity/Tithe

Chart 23-1

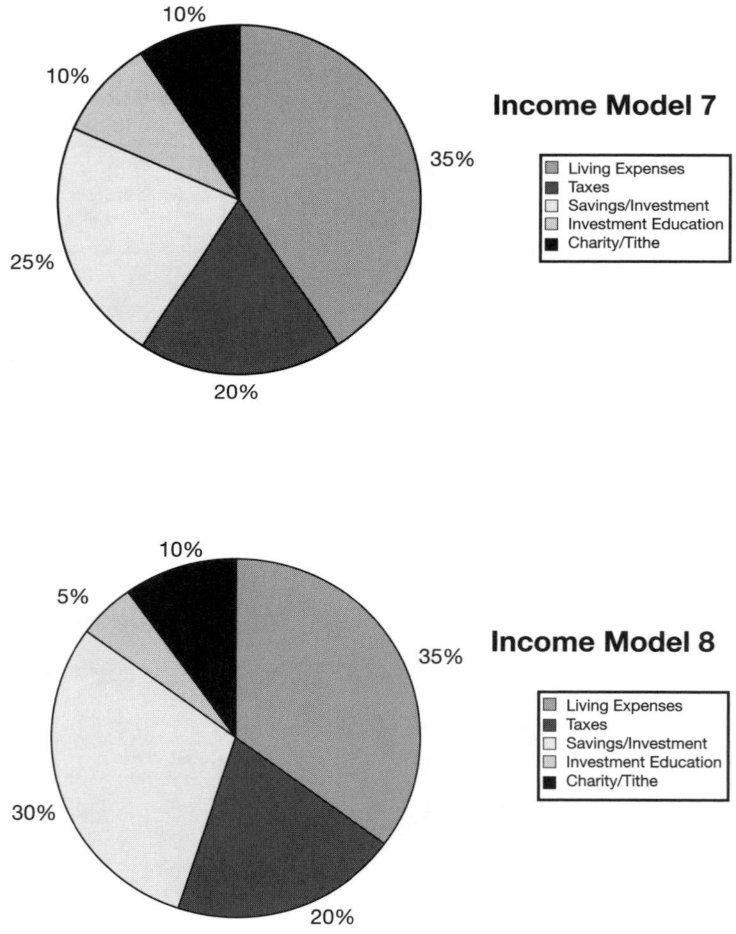
10%
10%
Income Model 7
35%
Living Expenses
Taxes
Savings/Investment
Investment Education
Charity/Tithe
25%
20%
10%
5%
Income Model 8
35%
Living Expenses
Taxes
Savings/Investment
Investment Education
Charity/Tithe
30%
20%

Chart 23-1

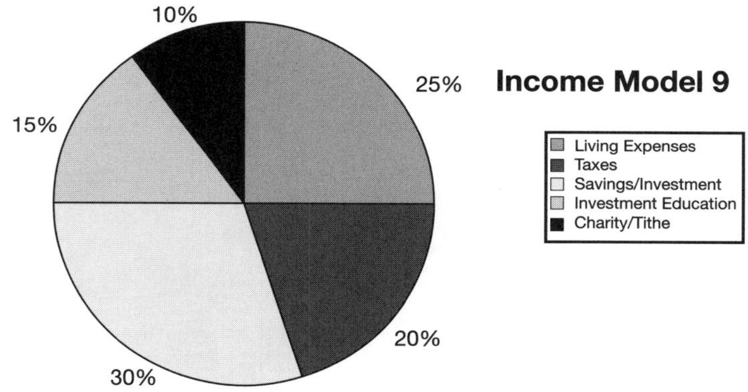
Income Model 9
10%
25%
15%
20%
30%
Living Expenses
Taxes
Savings/Investment
Investment Education
Charity/Tithe

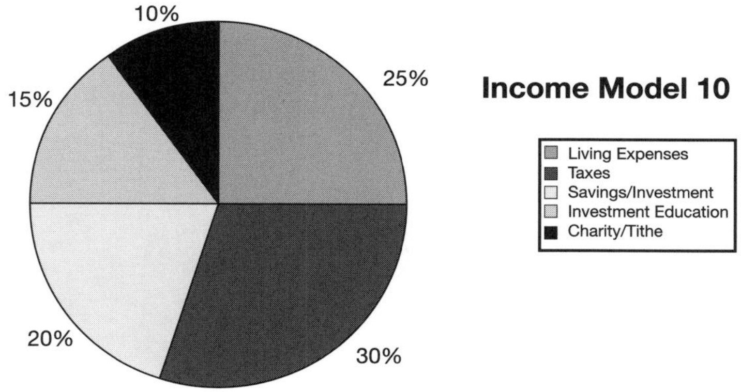
Income Model 10
10%
25%
15%
20%
30%
Living Expenses
Taxes
Savings/Investment
Investment Education
Charity/Tithe

Chapter 24

The Millionaire Business Structure

Whenever you see a successful business, someone once made a courageous decision.

Peter Drucker

For the majority of readers, starting a business will be a mandatory part of accumulating enough wealth to reach your Millionaire Goal. Though a small percentage of employees, usually high-income executives, can reach their Millionaire Goal without establishing a business entity, most will need to do so at some point. Most will own stock as at least a minority stockholder in some company. Another likely scenario is that the millionaire-minded business executive may resign from employment at some point and go into business for him or herself.

What type of organized business entity structure are you going to use to run your millionaire wealth business plan? There are several types of business entity structures and each has its benefits as well as its "red tape" in the beginning. Many of the more precarious moments can be avoided if you are running at full speed.

Remember, you need to use all available resources to help strengthen your mindset if you are serious about building wealth and a million-dollar net worth. You will never be successful if you cut corners, especially if you choose to invest in starting your own business, because your business can end up looking like no more than a project that you do in your spare time. There is a difference between a part-time business plan and something that you do in your spare time. If you are doing things right, you probably won't have much spare time. You can build a successful business with a part-time business plan. What type of entity will you choose? The following shows the different types of business entity choices that are available.

The Sole Proprietorship:

The simplest type of business to run is a sole proprietorship. If you name your business after yourself, using only your first name, last name, or both (e.g., Robert Garcia), and have no employees, you don't have to file an "assume name certificate" or obtain a new employer identification number (EIN) from the IRS. If you use a name that is different from your own name, you will have to file an "assume name certificate" in each county where you conduct business. If your business employs persons other than yourself, you will need to obtain an EIN from the IRS. You will simply file a schedule C with your IRS 1040 income tax return to report your sales, cost of goods sold, and expenses, then put your net profit or loss on your IRS 1040 page one and pay income taxes and self-employment social security taxes on your total self-employment income.

Although this is the easiest type of business entity, all liabilities rest on your shoulders. You and the business entity are now one and the same. Creditors can come after you individually for any debts, obligations, or liabilities of the business. Lawsuits can be filed against you and your business. A sole proprietorship may offer the least amount of tax write-offs and deductions, depending on your net profits.

The Partnership:

You and your partner can combine twice the resources, including capital and time, to help the business grow twice as fast. A partnership is probably the least used type of business entity being utilized today, mainly because (a) one partner may do more work and earn more profits than the other, and (b) each partner is legally responsible for the other's actions, and can be financially responsible for all of the debts, obligations, and liabilities of the partnership.

The Subchapter S-Corporation:

There are two features enjoyed by subchapter S-corporations that offer great benefits at the start. The first is that the business itself is a separate entity that is not attached to your personal assets and liabilities, because the corporation structure allows for limited liability to its shareholders. Second, the subchapter S-corporation tax reporting rules require that all profits or losses reported on its 1120-S tax return pass through the corporate entity to the individual shareholder's personal IRS 1040 income tax return.

The C-Corporation:

The C-corporation is like a public corporation in that it will file a separate IRS 1120 tax return reporting its own sales and expenses and its own profits or losses. You will also file your own individual IRS 1040 tax return to report any salaries, bonuses, or dividends you receive as the primary or only stockholder. It carries many tax-deductible benefits that can be used by the owners, including medical plans, retirement plans, and special benefits. Any dividends paid to the stockholders are taxable on their personal IRS 1040 tax return and are subject to a second round of income taxation. But, it does have many tax-deductible features not found in other entities.

The Limited Liability Company (LLC):

The limited liability company, or LLC, is a type of business entity that will protect the owners' or members' liability exposure through the limited liability feature. The LLC can choose how it files its tax return: through an IRS form 1040, schedule C, like a sole proprietorship (if there is only one member), an IRS form 1065, like a partnership (if there is more than one member), or an IRS form 1120 or 1120-S, like a corporation (if it files an IRS form 8832 "Choice of Entity" election to be taxed as an association).

You have many choices in establishing your business entity. Your tax professional and attorney team members can help you set up the right entity for you, as well as make sure that you are fully compliant with state law requirements and IRS standards. Many owners of good businesses get into trouble with the IRS because they didn't know that they had to pay quarterly income taxes and payroll taxes. Unfortunately, the IRS does not consider "I didn't know" a valid reason for not paying your taxes. When you set up your business entity books correctly from the beginning, your business sales, and therefore your profits, can grow faster. So it pays to do it right the first time.

Now that you have chosen your business entity, what kind of business are you going to run? There are thousands of businesses to choose from. Will you run a traditional retail business and use a storefront to sell your goods? Or, will you have a franchised business with a turnkey business plan, and pay a royalty fee to the franchise owners? How about a network marketing business in which you distribute products or services to the consumer at either the wholesale or retail level? Can you sell your products or services on the Internet? You will need to research all of the different business types and find the one with a prosperous future that you can believe in.

Remember that although a business can produce the highest return on your investment, it can also carry the most risk. Do your homework. Research everything before you make a decision. Create a business plan only after you have found the right business for you. See Chart 27-1 for a sample business plan. You can do your business plan after you have set up your business entity. Some will wait to do a business plan only when they are seeking additional financing, but the sooner you do the business plan, the sooner your success will come.

Hispanic Millionaire Action Item:
Set up your business entity within
the next ninety days.

Chapter 25

The Infopreneur Business Model

The men who have done big things are those who were not afraid to attempt big things, and who were not afraid to risk failure in order to gain success.

B.C. Forbes

There is one other type of business model that I did not mention earlier. It is known as an "infopreneur business." It is one of the most recent types of business plans. It is the business of marketing and selling information. One of my dreams and long-term goals was to write a book. This book, my first book, is the culmination of that dream. You bought this book in order to receive the information on its pages. Do you have a book inside you, waiting to come out? I believe everyone has at least one good book in them. Go for it.

How do you market and sell information? There are many ways to sell information. If you look at Chart 25-1, you will see a list of infopreneur business ideas. The benefit of selling information is that the "product" is in near limitless supply. It's constantly being generated. You have a world of information at your fingertips; all you have to do is decide how to organize, produce, and market it.

Study the following list of infopreneur subjects. Which subjects and services might hold the most interest for Hispanic-Americans or Americans in general?

Success and Maturation	Entrepreneurship
Headaches	Advertising
Time Management	Marketing
Sales Training	Computer Services
Stress	Financial Analysis
Fitness	Weight Loss
Cooking	Internet

What about specializing in services that are offered only to other infopreneurs?

Internet Webmaster	Mailing List Broker
Electronic Services	Info Marketing Coach
Speech Coach	Video Reproduction
Library Agent	Audio Producer
Infomercial Producer	Public Relations

The key to a thriving infopreneur business is building a million-dollar database and creating a lifelong relationship with your customers and/or clients. For example, an author of books on financial information could market his "product" through bookstores like Barnes & Noble, through Internet stores like Amazon.com, and through his own Website, which he promotes via carefully targeted E-mails. He might also market his book in audio form. Finally, he might offer seminars and workshops that expand on the information in his books.

Your customers will pay a fortune for information that they need today. Do research on companies that will be your main competitors; find out about their prices, marketing, target market, and anything else that would give you a leg up. Now, can you sell similar information at a lower cost or add more services for the same price? How will you find your customers? You might advertise on the Internet, TV, or radio, mail letters, send post cards, give seminars, or attend business expos. Select a topic of information that you have a passion for, research it, find out who will buy it, set up your database, package your product, and start marketing it. Have fun!

Hispanic Millionaire Action Item:
Get a notebook and divider tabs and begin writing your book.

Chart 25-1

Infopreneur Business Ideas

___Book Author	___Computer CD-ROM Sales
___Publishing	___TV Producer
___Seminar Sales	___Personal Consultant
___Public Speaker	___Professor/Teacher/Trainer
___Telecommunications	___Freelance Writer
___Newsletters	___Calendar Creator
___E-Books	___Internet Expert
___Audio-CDs	___Reports
___Manuals	___Home Study
___Videos	___Posters
___Journals	___Magazines
___Teleconferencing	___Radio
___Chat Rooms	___Movies

Chapter 26

Internet Marketing

Opportunity is missed by most people because it is dressed in overalls and looks like work.

Thomas A. Edison

Did you realize that it is possible to make $1,000,000 (yes, one million dollars!) a year via the Internet? In fact, some people make that amount in one month, or even in one week. Many successful entrepreneurs have taken a product or service and generated millions of dollars by selling it on the Internet. How many business opportunities make money for you while you sleep? How much money could you make if you made 10 cents from each person who uses the Internet? What if you made $500 from one-tenth of 1 percent of all Internet users? The Internet is an awesome tool. It is like having the whole world in your home office. There are many different business opportunities and successful strategies to help you make income on the Internet.

To understand the basics of Internet marketing, you must first realize that simply creating a Webpage is not enough. Your Webpage may look very professional, be decorated with beautiful colors and fancy pop-up menus . . . and do nothing to create an Internet-based profit. You must design your Website to sell, and that means starting with a concrete idea of how your product or service will do in the market. Imagine yourself visiting the Website for the first time with an interest in purchasing the products listed. What would you need to see? What site design or product descriptions would make you want to spend your hard-earned money? If you search the Internet, it won't take long to find hundreds of confusing Websites. They may be difficult to buy items from or may even be impossible to navigate.

If you are interested in creating a successful Internet business, I recommend that you go to the "One-Hour Hispanic Millionaire" Website, click on "Webpage design," and use our affiliate program wholesaler to purchase and produce your own Website. We provide the equivalent of a ready-made business and marketing plan to help sell your products. Once you have an Internet business marketing plan for your online business, you can focus on giving your Webpage the right colors, fonts, graphics, designs, pop-ups, ordering forms, sales letters, and product descriptions. I want you to go from point A to point B, not from point A to point X as many people do. With your professional Website up and running, how will you help all of those potential customers find you?

Your Website

How do you get people to your site? There are many ways to attract people and get them to visit your Website. I will discuss several here. The first way is by marketing your Website address. You should put your Website address on everything you print to help market your business. Put it on your business cards, stationery, envelopes, bumper stickers, even every E-mail message you send. You can also put your Web address on greeting cards, wedding gifts, on your voice mail message . . . everything.

The second way is through the use of search engines. Remember, it is easier to sell products to customers if they find you themselves by going to your Website or if they E-mail you for additional information on a particular product or service. Why? Simply because they are looking for the type of product or service you are marketing. They have "chosen" you and that's always good! You will need online search engine companies to send traffic to your site. Go to www.onehourhispanicmillionaire.com, click on "search engines," and it will lead you to the top search engines in the United States. A typical search could generate thousands, if not millions, of results. Therefore, your goal should be to appear at or near the top of that long, long, loooooong list. There are at least three ways to help you find the right search engine: 1) Go to every major search engine and submit your Webpage and then start praying that they will back you. 2) Hire a company that will do the work for you by submitting your Webpage to every search engine in the known Internet universe. 3) Find a company that you can afford that has produced satisfactory to average results. You can also find companies that are willing to charge you on a "per click" basis, or the number of times people visit your site. You have absolute control over what kind of hits (keywords, etc.) you receive and how much you will spend each week or each month.

The third way of getting prospects to your Website is by putting an advertisement in an E-zine. Your ad will be read by a large audience who may already be interested in your particular product. It's similar to advertising in a national printed magazine. You can also buy or rent E-mail mailing lists. You will want to rent E-mail mailing lists where the people on the list have already "opted in" and agreed to receive ads from online businesses. There are lists of E-mail address holders from all over the country or from your specific region. Use these lists to mail direct marketing packages offering them a special report or gift if they are willing send their E-mail address to your Website. Your goal is to build an E-mail database that is so extensive that each time you send out a mass offer (remember, it's free), you increase your odds of generating sales. When you have a large E-mail database, the right search engines with your Website listed, and the E-zine ads that work for your products, you will have created the opportunity to reach your million-dollar goals. Another way to make money on the Internet, even if you have no products or services, is through affiliate programs. You set up an affiliate program with one or more companies, and each company pays you a commission for each product that is sold through your Website. You can have as many affiliate programs as you want. The other part of making revenue through affiliate programs is doing follow-up E-mail marketing. You send E-mails to all of the people who bought the affiliate's product.

Your fortune can be made if you follow prospects, sell existing products, create Internet ads, and even create new products in the future. When you are assembling your Master Mind group, you should add a reputable technology or Internet coordinator to your team.

Hispanic Millionaire Action Item:
Set up a Webpage and then start playing with different designs and formats.

Chart 26-1

Internet Marketing Checklist

- ________ What Do You Want to Market/Sell?
- ________ What Are You an Expert At?
- ________ Who Is Your Competition?
- ________ Write a Business Plan.
- ________ Create a Logo and/or Brand Name.
- ________ Determine Your Target Market.
- ________ Domain Name(s).
- ________ Web Hosting.
- ________ Designing Your Website.
- ________ Your Sales Letter or Copy.
- ________ Your Unique Selling Proposition (USP).
- ________ Catalog.
- ________ Automate.
- ________ Credit Card and Checks Acceptance.
- ________ International Orders.
- ________ Your "Shopping Cart."
- ________ Delivering Your Products.
- ________ Sales and Guarantees to Customers.
- ________ Fraud Protection.
- ________ Charge Backs, Yes.
- ________ Newsletter—Free/Charge.
- ________ E-mail Addresses Collection.
- ________ Storing E-mail Addresses.
- ________ Buying E-mail Lists.
- ________ Search Engines.
- ________ Directories.
- ________ Classified Ads.
- ________ E-mail Marketing.
- ________ No Spam.
- ________ Automating Your E-mails.
- ________ Auto Responses.
- ________ Testing and Tracking Your Strategies.

Chapter 27

Leveraging Business Capital

To get profit without risk, experience without danger and reward without work is as impossible as it is to live without being born.

A.P. Gouthey

There are two kinds of debts: consumer debt and business debt. Consumer debt is the kind of debt that can get you in trouble. My advice is, don't go there. I'm not saying that you can't "have" the consumer goods you want and need; just resist the temptation to finance them. You should plan more for your consumer purchases, and it is more profitable to you to pay consumer debt quickly, or save the money and pay cash.

On the other hand, business loans or capital can leverage your profits and wealth immensely. When you are borrowing money to increase your sales and profits, then it is a good business loan. Now, don't even think that all business loans turn into profits. It doesn't work that way. That is why it is very important to have a business and marketing plan before you borrow or set up a business. Go to Chart 27-1 for a sample business plan. While you can save money for a startup and build your business slowly, a good business loan can double or even quadruple your sales and profits. The equipment, working capital, staff support, and so on has to come either from your savings account, your regular cash flow, or from a business loan.

There are several reasons many businesses fail in their first five years. One of the major causes of failure is inadequate capitalization, or underfunding. Every business has a formula for what equals their gross sales and profits based on their percent of capitalization. One businessowner may be very happy to make $50,000 a year with no more loans, while another business may need capitalization to increase profits to $100,000. When you borrow for your business startup or to expand your existing business, you need to know where every dollar is going. You need to know how many new dollars it will create. Business capital/loans can return 2-1, 5-1, or 25-1 for each dollar borrowed.

There are many ways to capitalize your business and many reasons you might need capital. We will first discuss the latter. You may need capital to:

Acquire more inventory to increase sales.
Handle increased accounts receivable due to new sales growth.
Take care of monthly expenses caused by new growth.
Buy larger or faster equipment to increase sales and decrease expenses.
Buy large amounts because of the substantial discount involved.
Make up the difference in revenues caused by decreased sales due to market conditions.
Account for your failure in saving money.
Infuse your business with more working capital.
Buy real estate (instead of leasing).

When an experienced and successful businessperson needs money, he or she will have no problem acquiring a new business loan.

It produces the payback of the loan, then interest on its use, and a profit to the business. An inexperienced businessowner can spend the loan proceeds unwisely and then continue to build a losing debt pool. So, what do you do if you need capital to start or to expand your business and work toward your wealth goals? What kinds of loans are available to you?

Let's start with Basic Financing 101. You can:

1. Sell some of your assets: jewelry, boats, and autos.
2. Take out a home equity loan.
3. Borrow against your retirement assets.
4. Get friends and family to invest in your company.
5. Use credit cards (admittedly, this is not the best option, but it will provide capital).

The next stage of financing, or your second source of capital, will come from a bank loan. If you already have a banker as a Master Mind team member and have done business with him or her before, he or she may be the only source of capital you need.

The third type of loan is through the Small Business Administration (SBA). You have probably heard about all the red tape involved in an SBA loan, but it doesn't take any longer than a conventional loan, as long as you have all the required documents. Why would you want to get an SBA loan versus a bank loan? There are several reasons. The first (and possibly only) one is that the bank will not lend you the money without an SBA guarantee (or wrap), in case of default of the loan. What happens is this: the SBA guarantees to the bank—or to a certified development company—a percentage of the total loan package. Other reasons for securing an SBA loan versus a bank loan include better interest terms/rates and longer payouts (lower payments) by the business.

The last type of business capital comes from an equity-based investor—a partner or stockholder who can receive part of the profits or interest from a loan. In many cases the loan or equity investment to the business can be structured as a loan with a higher interest charge and payable at a future date, or based on a percentage of gross sales in the form of a lump sum payment. Some loans may require interest payback as well as profits from the business until an agreed-upon buyout is settled. For smaller investments (less than $1 million) an *angel investor* may be found. The angel investor is looking to make better returns than he or she could get from a traditional investment portfolio. Some angel investors may charge a higher interest rate or ask for a greater percentage of the profits than you feel comfortable with. It's your choice. Sometimes you have to walk away from an investor, and that's okay. Do what feels right to you.

Hispanic Millionaire Action Item:

Write a business plan every year.

Chart 27-I

Sample Business Plan

I. Business Summary
Your mission statement, objectives, and keys to success for the business.

II. Company Summary
What type of business entity (sole proprietorship, corporation, etc.), the history of business, any sales and profit history, and where business is located.

III. Services and Products
Describe your current products or services, future products and services, costs, sales price, literature, why your products and services are needed, and why customers will buy from you.

IV. Marketing Plan and Analysis
What market segments will you be marketing to? What are the needs of this market? How big is your market? What are future trends in your market? What is the future growth of your market segments? How will you distribute your products and services to this market? Who is your competition?

V. Website Plan
What will be your Website marketing plan? Will you offer product and service information, ordering from Website, E-mail sign-up, and/or sales letters?

VI. Sales and Promotional Strategy
You should include all the projected costs and expenses for marketing your products and services. What types of advertising—newspaper, radio, brochures, TV, sales letters, postcards, Internet marketing costs, and/or joint venture marketing or affiliate programs? Project your sales, cost of goods sold, gross profit, expenses, salaries, and taxes for three to five years. You will probably have to do these projections several times. That's okay, the more you do, the better your forecast for a successful business.

VII. Business Management and Personnel
Draw up an organizational chart showing each position in your business. Then describe what each position will do. What will be compensation for each employee—salary or commissions, or both? Will any outside investors be involved with investment of money or time?

VIII. Cash Flow and Balance Sheet Statements
Cash flow and balance sheet statements are better forecasting tools than just a projected sales forecast. You will find out very quickly if you will have any cash or assets to carry on if your forecast is wrong. A cash flow pro-forma includes cash received for sales, sales tax received, new loans received, expenses from all categories, accounts payable, loan re-payments—anything that will show cash coming in or going out of your business. The balance sheet statement shows your business assets and liabilities and net worth on a month-to-month basis.

Chapter 28

Wealth and Asset Protection

It is not manly to turn one's back on fortune.

Marcus Annaeus Seneca

We have said throughout this entire book that through proper pre-planning you can achieve your financial and wealth goals. It's true. You *can* become a millionaire by taking action on your personal financial plan. Unfortunately, your newfound wealth creates a whole new problem: there are plenty of "predators" out there who are only too happy to take it off your hands. Since the majority of Hispanic-Americans have never reached those wealth goals, asset and wealth portfolios are thought of as something that is only for the "rich." However, I can assure you that any degree of savings, investments, or real estate ownership can be taken from you by just one lawsuit. You need to protect your wealth from anyone who wants to take it from you.

There are numerous strategies for building a "financial fortress" around your assets. If you have built your "Master Mind" team of advisors, you should have an asset protection attorney to help you protect your wealth. This is absolutely critical. If you doubt it, consider the fact that *someone is sued in America every minute.* Of all the lawsuits that are filed in the world, more than 90 percent are filed in the United States.

We will review several types of asset and wealth protection strategies. Some of the strategies I have already mentioned or discussed in other chapters for other reasons. The more strategies you set up, the more protection you will have for your assets. Never forget that the wealth that you spent so many years and so much hard work accumulating can be taken from you overnight. It is actually easier to make money than it is to keep it. As your wealth increases, your enemies or demons will also multiply.

Your best action is to meet with your advisor attorney and write each legal document for your protection. The majority of middle-income Hispanic-Americans—and even some wealthy ones—hesitate to sit with an attorney because of the fees. This is another mindset you will need to conquer. It could cost you millions if you don't set up your "fortress" properly.

I can tell you that in my personal situation, for my own asset protection planning, that fees were also an issue. If you still are thinking about the cost of the legal fees, you still have the mindset of being broke, or doing every plan yourself. When I first met attorney Peter Parenti, who is board certified in tax law, estate planning, and probate law, he was on the board of the International Association of Financial Planners (IAFP). At that time we were using several attorneys to advise my clients. I liked Peter right away because he is not only an expert in asset protection estate planning, but he is also an expert implementer of living trust estate plans and asset protection estate plans. Peter is the author and originator of The Living Trust in Texas. He is a marketing attorney. He did not wait for referrals from any advisors; he went to work and marketed directly to the client. I will tell you that any work Peter does for you is either the best or equal to the best. Many of the following asset and wealth protection models came from meetings between Peter and me, for my own asset protection plan and for the plans of my clients.

Business Entity

We talked earlier about the different forms of setting up your business entity. Your first asset protection plan will come from setting up the proper entity for your traditional business or home business—outside of your personal assets—primarily, an S-corporation, C-corporation, or an LLC (limited liability company).

Insurance Protection

Liability Insurance: *Liability insurance* is actually the easiest and often the most overlooked asset protection vehicle. Although many people cling to a "the cheaper, the better" mindset, it is preferable to increase your coverage and have higher deductibles. Experts would say that your auto liability insurance limits should be increased to at least $300,000 to $500,000. You should increase your *homeowners liability* insurance coverage (enough to cover a home business if needed). You should also consider acquiring at least $1,000,000 of *umbrella liability* coverage. Seek out *business liability* and/or *jumbo liability* policies. Your *medical insurance* maximum should be the highest you are offered or can afford, whether it comes from your employer, your spouse's employer, or your own business medical insurance.

Life Insurance: How much *life insurance* do you really need? Questions you have to ask yourself are: *What do I want to do for my family if I die? Should my spouse continue to work, even though one parent has died? What amount of income do I want to provide for my spouse and children for the rest of their lives?* Everyone has different goals and objectives for their families. You have two decisions to make: the first decision is from the heart and the second decision is from your income or assets. You will have to make the first decision on your own. The second decision will have to come from calculating the loss of your life as an asset that produces income and wealth for your family.

To replace your income, you will have to calculate how much income you will produce for your family for a certain period of time, say twenty years or fifty years, or whatever you estimate to be your life expectancy. You will also need to figure in an amount that will be needed to pay off your debts and taxes, and an amount for any important charitable donations. We have found that most people don't realize that they themselves are assets that produce income and that this asset has a replacement value. Then you also have to add in an inflation factor to account for the increase in your income stream over time. An easy example would show that if a person were making $50,000 in annual income, he would need to provide his family with an asset value of about $1,000,000 if it produces a 5 percent return, or an asset value of $625,000 if it produces an 8 percent return. Then you have to figure in the inflation projection, which would increase both of the asset values in the above example.

Disability Income Insurance: The next type of insurance product is *disability income insurance*. This is insurance to replace your salary or business income if you should become disabled and can no longer work or be productive. It can replace only earned income, not investment income. Usually there is a coverage maximum of 60 to70 percent of one's salary or earned income that most insurance companies will use when providing disability income insurance.

Long-Term Care Insurance: Long-Term Care (LTC) insurance is the newest type of insurance coverage. LTC insurance will pay for long-term health care at home or in a nursing home. Contrary to popular belief, long-term health care is not covered by health insurance or Medicare. Medicaid will pay for LTC, provided that you can prove that you are "broke." LTC insurance covers what medical insurance will not cover. Medical insurance will not cover what is referred to as the "activities of daily living" (ADL). ADL includes bathing, dressing, toileting, transferring, eating, and continence. Usually LTC policies will pay if you are expected to need help for at least ninety days with two or more activities on the ADL list.

Qualified Retirement Plans

Qualified retirement plans are considered "qualified" because the contributions to these plans are qualified for a tax deduction under Subchapter D of Chapter One of the Internal Revenue Code of 1986. There are also trusts and many good retirement plans that contain what is called a "spendthrift provision." A spendthrift provision prohibits the beneficiary of the trust from alienating or assigning his or her interest in the trust and prohibits the creditors of a beneficiary from invading the trust to satisfy their claims against the beneficiary. Qualified retirement plan benefits are also protected from the claims of a beneficiary's creditors under the federal law known as The Employees Retirement Income Security Act of 1974 (ERISA). Most of the states have also passed statutes that protect retirement plans from the claims of creditors.

We discussed earlier in the book the tax advantages of retirement plans and their leverage for investment return. A deferred annuity is similar to a qualified retirement plan and can also be a creditor-proof asset. Most deferred annuities are called Non-Qualified Retirement plans, and most states have passed laws allowing annuities to be creditor-proof also. You will need to check your state's law for qualification of this protection. Both types of retirement plans can be a "wealth storage box" for your accumulated assets.

Trusts

There are several types of trusts to choose from, depending on your family and your business goals. One of the easiest trusts to set up, and the first one you should have, is the revocable living trust. A revocable living trust can provide you and your family with the following benefits:

1. Allows the avoidance of probate
2. Remains a private estate planning document during your life and at your death

3. Provides savings on death taxes
4. Ensures total control of your assets that are owned by your living trust
5. Lets you designate who will manage your affairs upon your incapacity
6. Ensures the protection of the wealth you leave your loved ones from creditors and divorce
7. Offers much flexibility
8. Is very hard to contest
9. Reduces the likelihood of having unintended heirs
10. Is legal and enforceable in every state
11. Avoids multiple states probate with a living trust
12. Is easy to maintain.

This living trust replaces your will, which is subject to probate and is public record. The living trust is your primary trust for you and your family. You can add many additional trusts. Visit with your team attorney and find out about all the different types of trusts. When you have done all of the above, you will be ready to look at your next asset protection planning tool: "the family limited partnership."

Family Limited Partnership (FLP)

A family limited partnership is a limited partnership where the general and the limited partners are family members. The FLP offers asset protection, protection from income taxes, and reduction of potential estate taxes at death. An FLP can also reduce the size of your estate by allowing you to give shares in the partnership to family members, while still providing you with 100 percent control over your assets. You, as the general partner, are in complete control over all aspects of the business or investments of the partnership.

If you go to the Website www.onehourhispanicmillionaire.com and click on "portfolio," you can print samples of the documents and an asset protection data form to complete before you sit down with your team attorney.

Hispanic Millionaire Action Item:
Set up your living trust this
month—don't wait.

Chart 28-1

Asset Protection and Estate Planning Documents

____________	Birth Certificate
____________	Marriage Certificate
____________	Military Discharge Papers
____________	Divorce Papers
____________	Passport
____________	Insurance Policies
____________	Stocks and Bonds
____________	Deeds and Mortgages
____________	Titles
____________	Wills
____________	Living Trusts
____________	Business Agreements
____________	Power of Attorney
____________	Trusts
____________	Tax Returns
____________	Family Limited Partnership

Chapter 29

The One-Hour Hispanic Millionaire Model

It is impossible to win the great prizes in life without running risks.

Theodore Roosevelt

We are going to outline several models for your Millionaire Goal. You should start on one model, and then after you gain knowledge and conviction and increase your goals, you may choose to move to another model. You will see in the final chapter that you will put down the year that you want to reach that model goal. Remember to use the projected inflation and tax factors that we have discussed. As you will see, we have included "infopreneuring" as a separate business entity or asset, even though it could fall under business equity. It is a new type of business entity, and you can have both types of business entities in your millionaire models.

Model 120

$1 million net worth today—$3 million in 20 years

1. Retirement and Tax Plans	$1,000,000
2. Mutual Funds and Stocks	$1,000,000
3. Real Estate	$500,000
4. Business Equity	$250,000
5. Infopreneuring	$250,000
Total—20 years	$3,000,000

Model 220

$2 million net worth today—$6 million in 20 years

1. Retirement and Tax Plans	$1,500,000
2. Mutual Funds and Stocks	$1,500,000
3. Real Estate	$1,500,000
4. Business Equity	$750,000
5. Infopreneuring	$750,000
Total—20 years	$6,000,000

Model 110

$1 million net worth today—$2 million in 10 years

1. Retirement and Tax Plans	$500,000
2. Mutual Funds and Stocks	$500,000
3. Real Estate	$500,000
4. Business Equity	$250,000
5. Infopreneuring	$250,000
Total—20 years	$2,000,000

Model 210

$2 million net worth today—$4 million in 10 years

1. Retirement and Tax Plans	$750,000
2. Mutual Funds and Stocks	$750,000
3. Real Estate	$1,500,000
4. Business Equity	$500,000
5. Infopreneuring	$500,000
Total—10 years	$4,000,000

Model 105

$1 million net worth today—$1.4 million in 5 years

1. Retirement and Tax Plans	$150,000
2. Mutual Funds and Stocks	$150,000
3. Real Estate	$750,000
4. Business Equity	$250,000
5. Infopreneuring	$100,000
Total—5 years	$1,400,000

Model 205

$2 million net worth today—$2.8 million in 5 years

1. Retirement and Tax Plans	$400,000
2. Mutual Funds and Stocks	$400,000
3. Real Estate	$1,000,000
4. Business Equity	$500,000
5. Infopreneuring	$500,000
Total—5 years	$2,800,000

The most important decision you will make today, or this month (I will give you your only break), is to choose a model. (Well, you'll want to discuss it with your spouse, of course.) It doesn't matter which model. As I stated at the beginning of this chapter, you can change your model anytime, but it may be more realistic to choose one whose goals take a longer time period to reach.

It is much easier to make an adjustment to change to a faster time period model because of your increased knowledge. If you do more deals, make more sales, and invest more money, you will get to the faster model goal. All of these models are on the Website www.onehourhispanicmillionaire.com, as well as blank model forms to fill out. Remember, you can make your own model using your own family goals. For example, you may want to create your own Model 107 because in seven years you will turn fifty and you want to be a millionaire by then. When you choose your model, you *will* stick to it until you get there, or else you'll make a change to a new model goal. You will not look back (or you will turn into a pillar of salt), and you *will* accomplish your goal by age fifty (or whatever landmark you choose). Go to Chart 29-1 and do your first year model now.

Hispanic Millionaire Action Item:
Choose a model today and start—
you can always change later.

Chart 29-1

____

Date

One-Hour Hispanic Millionaire Model

Retirement & Tax Plans	$____________
Mutual Funds & Stocks	$____________
Real Estate	$____________
Business Equity	$____________
Infopreneuring	$____________
Total	$____________

Chapter 30

Your Million-Dollar Action Plan

Nothing great was ever achieved without enthusiasm.

Ralph Waldo Emerson

You and your spouse will want to read this chapter twice: once to see what you're committing to, and the second time to implement every action step. With that in mind, you should do this action plan when you are both fresh and under the least amount of stress. "Do not pass 'go,' do not collect $200—or $1,000,000, to be more accurate—until you do each step in sequence."

Action Step 1

You can print all the forms and charts you will need from www.onehourhispanicmillionaire.com. Fill out your Wealth Chart and Cash Flow Chart.

Action Step 2

Do a debt management analysis on all your debts and loans. Start with your mortgage balance and then do your loans and credit card balances. Use the formula in the book to project the number of months/years it will take to pay off your debts. If you implement the new home real estate strategy, you do not need to pay off your current mortgage, but do check to make sure you are paying the lowest rate for which you qualify.

Action Step 3

Choose your millionaire model from the six models in Chapter 29 or create your own. Figure out with your advisors what you have to do to fulfill each one of the five investment type goals, year by year, to reach your model goal.

Action Step 4

Figure out the amount of money you and your spouse can save on a monthly basis. Figure out the amount before taxes as well as after taxes (say, 10 percent, live on 90 percent). Take the 10 percent number and implement the following: (a) Put 50 percent of that 10 percent into your cash savings until you have six months of your salary in that account; (b) Until you've accumulated the six months of salary, use the other 50 percent to maximize your retirement and tax plans, whether you have a matching employee plan or only your contributions. If you have no employer plan, you will need to set up an IRA or SEP-IRA for yourself. After you've reached the six-months-salary milestone, you can start putting 100 percent of your savings into your retirement account; (c) When you have reached the goal of maximizing your retirement plans—which may take a few years—you can set up a plan for investing in mutual funds and stocks on a monthly or annual basis.

Action Step 5

You need to do your first real estate deal ASAP. Remember, the most important goal of real estate investing is to write that first contract. If you are ready to implement and are qualified, you can sell your present home and buy a new home with minimal down-payment and costs and invest the rest of your equity. After you implement your home deal, you can start looking for your first real estate investment and make an offer. Get with your realtor for help and expertise. Do a deal, but give yourself a way out if there are problems.

Action Step 6

Set up your asset and wealth protection plan. Contact your Master Mind team members for your insurance, estate, and asset protection. It is very important to set up your asset protection plan before you need to use it. Also, building wealth and making money requires that your frame of mind and your outer structure are set up for success. If not, your mind will block you from reaching your wealth goals.

Action Step 7

Set up your corporation or limited liability company, and start the process of investigating what your business will be.

Action Step 8

Write your business plan for your new or existing business. Will you need capital or not? Will you sell from a store, from your home business, or from the Internet? Once you have completed your business plan, you can begin selling products or services for a profit.

Action Step 9

Do a business plan on your infopreneur business. Now you may have two or three businesses with your big business plan. You may have a traditional non-Internet business but expand to offer monthly information on that business, or any other types of business, online. You may also sell your products and services strictly on the Internet.

Action Step 10

Believe it or not, once you reach step ten, you are on your way to success. You just have to repeat the steps, monthly, quarterly, and semi-annually, to reach your model goals. As you repeat each step, you will make adjustments. Taking action, repeating, and making any adjustments to your millionaire success plan will help to get you to your goal. Finally, remember you are an American living in the United States and you have the greatest opportunities for wealth accumulation and millionaire success available anywhere. You are an American and you are entitled to take advantage of every opportunity that is offered. There are no ethnic or cultural barriers to success, only those you create yourself or allow others to create for you. You are a Hispanic-American—or, if you don't like hyphens, an *American*—and you have the freedom to become a millionaire. You *will* become a millionaire.

Hispanic Millionaire Action Item:
Outline this book chapter by chapter, and
read it again, until your actions
become a habit.

Chart 30-1

One-Hour Hispanic Millionaire Monthly Checklist

____________	Mindset Books
____________	Millionaire Books
____________	Net Worth Chart
____________	Earnings Chart
____________	Acres of Diamonds Checklist
____________	Wealth Chart—Balance Sheet
____________	Wealth Chart—Income Sheet
____________	Debt Chart
____________	Tax Bracket
____________	Planning Goals Chart
____________	Calendar
____________	Team Professionals
____________	Home Goals Chart
____________	Income Plan
____________	Business Structure
____________	Infopreneur Model
____________	Internet Model
____________	Business Plan
____________	OHHM Model
____________	Action Plan

Other Ways to Learn from Ruben Ruiz:

You've just read a wealth of insights from Ruben Ruiz, MSFS, ChFC, on reinventing your mindset, your lifestyle, and ultimately, your bank account. If you found *The One-Hour Hispanic Millionaire* inspiring and educational, you may wish to share his message with others. He offers his services as a keynote speaker and workshop leader to businesses and organizations of all types and sizes.

CEO of The Ruiz Financial Group, LLC, Ruiz draws on his thirty years of experience in the financial planning, financial services, insurance, and investment industries to teach audiences how to set financial goals and acquire long-term wealth. His keynote presentations answer questions like: *Why am I not wealthy when other Americans with similar backgrounds are? What does it take to be a millionaire? Must I have a certain educational background? Certain types of work experience? What is the secret that everyone but me seems to know?*

Ruiz speaks and conducts workshops on the following topics:

- How to create an investment portfolio with the least risk and most return
- How to turn your business into a wealth investment
- How to write a business plan
- How to set up a college plan for your children and grandchildren
- How to protect your assets through proper risk management
- How to make the IRS your partner, not your tax collector
- How to turn your home into a half-million-dollar tax-free return
- How to understand the miracle of investment compounding

People who attend Ruiz's keynotes or workshops regularly learn wealth-building secrets and insights such as:

- How your "computer mind" can start you on the road to wealth
- How to chart a road map to your financial goals
- How to avoid the fallacy of "getting rich overnight" and start thinking at the beginning
- How to recognize the importance of taking one step at a time (learning the alphabet...then words...then sentences...then story)
- How to make planning—weekly, then daily—an integral part of your life
- How to quit thinking "cheap" in your purchases and investments
- How to create a Master Mind team to help you meet your wealth goals
- How to master the five demons of building wealth
- How to understand the four wealth-building quadrants

To book Ruben Ruiz for a keynote presentation or workshop, call 210-573-6827, visit www.onehourhispanicmillionaire.com, or E-mail ruben@onehourhispanicmillionaire.com or rruiz@grandecom.net.

About the Author

Ruben Ruiz Jr., MSFS, CLU, ChFC, CSA, RFC, is regional director and financial advisor of Money Concepts Financial Planning Centres in San Marcos and San Antonio, Texas, and CEO of The Ruiz Financial Group, LLC. He was recently elected to the International Association of Registered Financial Consultants Board of Directors. Ruben's firms have a long tradition of helping clients build, manage, and protect their wealth through financial planning and investment advisory services, with an emphasis on college funding and retirement planning. Ruben's clients consist principally of high-net-worth individuals, baby-boomers, and business owners.

A dedicated financial professional since 1974, Ruben speaks with enthusiasm: "My mission is to provide my clients with the finest financial planning and advisory services available in the United States today, in order to help them maintain their family values and achieve their family goals."

Ruben earned his master of science in financial services (MSFS) degree from the Richard D. Irwin Graduate School of The American College, Bryn Mawr, Pennsylvania.

Ruben holds a bachelor of business administration (BBA) degree from Southwest Texas State University (Texas State University) and has earned the professional designations of chartered life underwriter (CLU) and chartered financial consultant (ChFC). In recognition of his professionalism he has been honored with memberships in the Money Concepts Millionaires Club, Eagles Club, Century Club, and

Professionals Club. In 1997 he received the coveted Financial Planner of the Year Bronze Award. Ruben received the "certified senior advisor" designation in 2001.

Ruben is a member of the Financial Planning Association (FPA) of San Antonio and South Texas, and has served in various positions for the organization, including president and chairman of the board for 1999-2000. He conducts seminars on financial topics and has published articles in local newspapers, as well as a column for the *San Marcos Record.*

In 1997, Ruben expanded his services to add mortgage loans. Currently Mr. Ruiz is an independent mortgage broker representing several lenders throughout the U.S.

Ruben is a member of the Texas State Alumni Association (SWT) and also holds several positions of responsibility in the community. A resident of central Texas with his wife, Amanda, and their two children, Richard and Raquel, he enjoys golfing, jogging, and fitness workouts.